ON THE WAY TO LANGUAGE

Harper & Row Editions of
MARTIN HEIDEGGER

Basic Writings
Being and Time
Discourse on Thinking
Early Greek Thinking
The End of Philosophy
Hegel's Concept of Experience
Identity and Difference
Nietzsche: Volume I, The Will to Power as Art
Nietzsche: Volume IV, Nihilism
On the Way to Language
On Time and Being
Poetry, Language, Thought
The Question Concerning Technology and Other Essays
What Is Called Thinking?

MARTIN HEIDEGGER

ON THE WAY TO LANGUAGE

Translated by PETER D. HERTZ

1817

HARPER & ROW, PUBLISHERS, San Francisco
Cambridge, Hagerstown, New York, Philadelphia
London, Mexico City, São Paulo, Sydney

Originally published by Verlag Günther Neske, Pfullingen, under the title Unterwegs zur Sprache, *copyright 1959 by Verlag Günther Neske.*

First Harper & Row paperback edition published in 1982.

Library of Congress Cataloging in Publication Data

Heidegger, Martin, 1889-1976.
    On the way to language.

    Translation of: Unterwegs zur Sprache.
    Includes bibliographical references.
    1. Languages—Philosophy.   I. Title.
P106.H3613   1982   401   77-124708
ISBN 0-06-063859-1 (pbk.)   AACR2

83   84   85   86   10   9   8   7   6   5   4   3   2

CONTENTS

A DIALOGUE ON LANGUAGE

A DIALOGUE ON LANGUAGE

between a Japanese and an Inquirer

Japanese: You know Count Shuzo Kuki. He studied with you for a number of years.

Inquirer: Count Kuki has a lasting place in my memory.

J: He died too early. His teacher Nishida wrote his epitaph— for over a year he worked on this supreme tribute to his pupil.

I: I am happy to have photographs of Kuki's grave and of the grove in which it lies.

J: Yes, I know the temple garden in Kyoto. Many of my friends often join me to visit the tomb there. The garden was established toward the end of the twelfth century by the priest Honen, on the eastern hill of what was then the Imperial city of Kyoto, as a place for reflection and deep meditation.

I: And so, that temple grove remains the fitting place for him who died early.

J: All his reflection was devoted to what the Japanese call *Iki.*

I: In my dialogues with Kuki, I never had more than a distant inkling of what that word says.

J: Later, after his return from Europe, Count Kuki gave lectures in Kyoto on the aesthetics of Japanese art and poetry. These lectures have come out as a book. In the book, he attempts to consider the nature of Japanese art with the help of European aesthetics.

I: But in such an attempt, may we turn to aesthetics?

J: Why not?

I: The name "aesthetics" and what it names grow out of European thinking, out of philosophy. Consequently, aesthetic consideration must ultimately remain alien to Eastasian thinking.

J: You are right, no doubt. Yet we Japanese have to call on aesthetics to aid us.

I: With what?

J: Aesthetics furnishes us with the concepts to grasp what is of concern to us as art and poetry.

I: Do you need concepts?

J: Presumably yes, because since the encounter with European thinking, there has come to light a certain incapacity in our language.

I: In what way?

J: It lacks the delimiting power to represent objects related in an unequivocal order above and below each other.

I: Do you seriously regard this incapacity as a deficiency of your language?

J: Considering that the encounter of the Eastasian with the European world has become inescapable, your question certainly calls for searching reflection.

I: Here you are touching on a controversial question which I often discussed with Count Kuki—the question whether it is necessary and rightful for Eastasians to chase after the European conceptual systems.

J: In the face of modern technicalization and industrialization of every continent, there would seem to be no escape any longer.

I: You speak cautiously, you say "... would seem..."

J: Indeed. For the possibility still always remains that, seen from the point of view of our Eastasian existence, the technical world which sweeps us along must confine itself to surface matters, and ... that ...

I: ... that for this reason a true encounter with European existence is still not taking place, in spite of all assimilations and intermixtures.

J: Perhaps cannot take place.

I: Can we assert this so unconditionally?

J: I would be the last to venture it, else I should not have come to Germany. But I have a constant sense of danger which Count Kuki, too, could obviously not overcome.

I: What danger are you thinking of?

J: That we will let ourselves be led astray by the wealth of concepts which the spirit of the European languages has in store, and will look down upon what claims our existence, as on something that is vague and amorphous.

I: Yet a far greater danger threatens. It concerns both of us; it is all the more menacing just by being more inconspicuous.

J: How?

I: The danger is threatening from a region where we do not suspect it, and which is yet precisely the region where we would have to experience it.

J: You have, then, experienced it already; otherwise you could not point it out.

I: I am far from having experienced the danger to its full extent, but I have sensed it—in my dialogues with Count Kuki.

J: Did you speak with him about it?

I: No. The danger arose from the dialogues themselves, in that they were dialogues.

J: I do not understand what you mean.

I: Our dialogues were not formal, scholarly discussions. Whenever that sort of thing seemed to be taking place, as in the seminars, Count Kuki remained silent. The dialogues of which I am thinking came about at my house, like a spontaneous game. Count Kuki occasionally brought his wife along who then wore festive Japanese garments. They made the Eastasian world more luminously present, and the danger of our dialogues became more clearly visible.

J: I still do not understand what you mean.

I: The danger of our dialogues was hidden in language itself, not in *what* we discussed, nor in the *way in which* we tried to do so.

J: But Count Kuki had uncommonly good command of German, and of French and English, did he not?

I: Of course. *He* could say in European languages whatever was under discussion. But we were discussing *Iki;* and here it was *I* to whom the spirit of the Japanese language remained closed—as it is to this day.

J: The languages of the dialogue shifted everything into European.

I: Yet the dialogue tried to *say* the essential nature of *Eastasian* art and poetry.

J: Now I am beginning to understand better where you smell the danger. The language of the dialogue constantly destroyed the possibility of saying what the dialogue was about.

I: Some time ago I called language, clumsily enough, the house of Being. If man by virtue of his language dwells within the claim and call of Being, then we Europeans presumably dwell in an entirely different house than Eastasian man.

J: Assuming that the languages of the two are not merely different but are other in nature, and radically so.

I: And so, a dialogue from house to house remains nearly impossible.

J: You are right to say "nearly." For still it was a dialogue—and, I should think, an exciting one, because Count Kuki, in the workshops he held with us at Kyoto University, came back again and again to those dialogues with you. Most often it happened when we pressed him in our effort to understand more clearly the reason that had prompted him at that time to go to Germany to study with you. Your book *Being and Time* had then not yet been published. But after the First World War several Japanese professors, among them our revered Professor Tanabe, went to Husserl, in Freiburg, to study phenomenology with him. That is how my compatriots came to know you in person.

I: It was just as you said. In those days I, as Husserl's assistant, regularly once a week read Husserl's first major work, the *Logical Investigations,* with the gentlemen from Japan. By that time the master himself no longer held his work in very high esteem; it had been published around the turn of the century. But I had my own reasons to prefer the *Logical Investigations* for the purposes of an introduction to phenomenology. And the master generously tolerated my choice.

J: At the time—I believe it was in 1921—our professors attended a class you gave. They brought a transcript of it back to Japan. The title, if I am not mistaken, was "Expression and Appearance."

I: That, in any event, was the title of the course. Yet Professor Kuki must have had his special reasons for coming to me in Marburg.

J: Indeed, and I believe these reasons trace back to that course whose transcript was also much discussed elsewhere in Japan.

I: Transcripts are muddy sources, of course; what is more, the course was most imperfect. Yet there was quickening in it the attempt to walk a path of which I did not know where it would lead. I knew only the most immediate short-range perspectives along that path, because they beckoned to me unceasingly, while the horizon shifted and darkened more than once.

J: My compatriots must indeed have sensed some of that. Again and again it was said that your questions circled around the problem of language and of Being.

I: In fact, this was not too difficult to discern; for as early as 1915, in the title of my dissertation "Duns Scotus' Doctrine of Categories and Theory of Meaning," the two perspectives came into view: "doctrine of categories" is the usual name of the discussion of the Being of beings; "theory of meaning" means the *grammatica speculativa,* the metaphysical reflection on language in its relation to Being. But all these relationships were then still unclear to me.

J: Which is why you kept silent for twelve years.

I: And I dedicated *Being and Time,* which appeared in 1927, to Husserl, because phenomenology presented us with possibilities of a way.

J: Still, it seems to me that the fundamental theme, "Language and Being," stayed there in the background.

I: It did stay there even in the course you mentioned, of 1921. The same held true also of the question of poetry, and of art. In those days of expressionism, these realms were constantly before me—but even more, and already since my student days before the First World War, was the poetic work of Hölderlin and Trakl. And still earlier, during my last years in the *Gymnasium*—to give a date, in the summer of 1907—I came up against the question of Being, in the dissertation of Husserl's teacher Franz Brentano. Its title is "On the manifold meaning of being according to Aristotle"; it dates from 1862. The book came to me as a gift from my fatherly friend and fellow Swabian, Dr. Conrad Gröber, later to become archbishop of Freiburg. Then he was vicar of Trinity Church in Constance.

J: Do you still have the book?

I: Here it is for you to look at, and to read the inscription which runs: "My first guide through Greek philosophy in my *Gymnasium* days." I am telling you all this, but not in order to give the impression that I already knew then everything that I am still asking today. But perhaps there is confirmation here for you—who as professor of German literature love and know Hölderlin's work particularly well—of a phrase of that poet which begins in the fourth stanza of the hymn "The Rhine": ". . . For as you began, so you will remain."

J: The quest of language and of Being is perhaps a gift of that light ray which fell on you.

I: Who would have the audacity to claim that such a gift has come to him? I only know one thing: because reflection on language, and on Being, has determined my path of thinking from early on, therefore their discussion has stayed as far as possible in the background. The fundamental flaw of the book *Being and Time* is perhaps that I ventured forth too far too early.

J: That can hardly be said of your thoughts on language.

I: True, less so, for it was all of twenty years after my doctoral dissertation that I dared discuss in a class the question of language. It was at that same time that I, in class, made public my first interpretations of Hölderlin's hymns. In the summer semester of 1934, I offered a lecture series under the title "Logic." In fact, however, it was a reflection on the *logos,* in which I was trying to find the nature of language. Yet it took nearly another ten years before I was able to say what I was thinking—the fitting word is still lacking even today. The prospect of the thinking that labors to answer to the nature of language is still veiled, in all its vastness. This is why I do not yet see whether what I am trying to think of as the nature of language is *also* adequate for the nature of the Eastasian language; whether in the end—which would also be the beginning—a nature of language can reach the thinking experience, a nature which would offer the assurance that European-Western saying and Eastasian saying will enter into dialogue such that in it there sings something that wells up from a single source.

J: But a source that would then still remain concealed from both language worlds.

I: That is what I mean. This is why your visit is especially welcome to me. Since you have already translated into Japanese a few of Kleist's plays, and some of my lectures on Hölderlin, you have a keener ear for the questions that I addressed to your compatriots almost thirty-five years ago.

J: You must not overestimate my abilities, especially since I, coming from Japanese poetry, still find it difficult to respond to European poetry in a way that does justice to its essential nature.

I: Even though the danger remains that is necessarily implied in our using the German language for our dialogue, I believe that I have meanwhile learned a little more, so that now I can ask questions better than several decades ago.

J: At that time, my compatriots' dialogues with you after class were taking a different direction.

I: Therefore I now ask you: what prompted the Japanese professors, and later in particular Count Kuki, to give special attention to that transcript?

J: I can report only of Kuki's explanations. They never did become fully clear to me; for, in characterizing your manner of thinking, he often invoked the terms "hermeneutics" and "hermeneutic."

I: As far as I remember, I first used those words in a later course, in the summer of 1923. That was the time when I began my first drafts of *Being and Time.*

J: In our judgment, Count Kuki did not succeed in explaining the terms satisfactorily, neither concerning the meaning of the word nor regarding the sense in which you were speaking of a hermeneutic phenomenology. Kuki merely stressed constantly that the term was to indicate a new direction of phenomenology.

I: It may indeed have looked that way. In fact, however, I was concerned neither with a direction in phenomenology nor, indeed, with anything new. Quite the reverse, I was trying to think the nature of phenomenology in a more originary manner, so as to fit it in this way back into the place that is properly its own within Western philosophy.

J: But why did you use the term "hermeneutic"?

I: The answer is given in the Introduction to *Being and Time* (Section 7C, pp. 58 ff.). But I will gladly add a few remarks, to dispel the illusion that the use of the term is accidental.

J: I recall that it was this illusion which caused objections.

I: The term "hermeneutics" was familiar to me from my theological studies. At that time, I was particularly agitated over the question of the relation between the word of Holy

Scripture and theological-speculative thinking. This relation, between language and Being, was the same one, if you
will, only it was veiled and inaccessible to me, so that
through many deviations and false starts I sought in vain
for a guiding thread.

J: I know too little of Christian theology to comprehend what
you refer to. But it is obvious that through your background and your studies you are at home in theology in a
manner totally different from those who come from outside and merely pick up through reading a few things that
belong in that area.

I: Without this theological background I should never have
come upon the path of thinking. But origin always comes
to meet us from the future.

J: If the two call to each other, and reflection makes its home
within that calling . . .

I: . . . and thus becomes true presence.—Later on, I met the
term "hermeneutic" again in Wilhelm Dilthey, in his theory
of the History of Ideas. Dilthey's familiarity with hermeneutics came from that *same* source, his theological studies
and especially his work on Schleiermacher.

J: As far as I am informed by philology, hermeneutics is a
science that deals with the goals, ways, and rules of the
interpretation of literary works.

I: It developed first and formatively in conjunction with the
interpretation of the Book of books, the Bible. There is a
lecture by Schleiermacher that was published posthumously
from his manuscripts under the title "Hermeneutics and
Criticism, with special reference to the New Testament"
(1838). I have it here, and shall read you the first two
sentences from the "General Introduction":

Hermeneutics and criticism, both philological disciplines, both
methodologies, belong together, because the practice of each

presupposes the other. The first is in general the art of understanding rightly another man's language, particularly his written language; the second, the art of judging rightly the genuineness of written works and passages, and to establish it on the strength of adequate evidence and data.

J: Accordingly, the word "hermeneutics," broadened in the appropriate sense, can mean the theory and methodology for every kind of interpretation, including, for example, that of works of the visual arts.

I: Quite.

J: Do you use the term in this broad sense?

I: If I may stay within the style of your question, I have to answer: In *Being and Time,* the term "hermeneutics" is used in a *still* broader sense, "broader" here meaning, however, not the mere extension of the same meaning over a still larger area of appplication. "Broader" is to say: in keeping with that vastness which springs from originary being. In *Being and Time,* hermeneutics means neither the theory of the art of interpretation nor interpretation itself, but rather the attempt first of all to define the nature of interpretation on hermeneutic grounds.

J: But what does "hermeneutic" mean then? I do not have the audacity to yield to the suspicion which here suggests itself, that you are now using the word "hermeneutic" willfully. Be that as it may, what matters to me is to hear from your own lips an—if I may say so—authentic explanation of your use of the word; otherwise it will still not become clear what moved Count Kuki's reflections.

I: I shall be glad to do as you ask. Only, do not expect too much. For the matter is enigmatic, and perhaps we are not dealing with a matter at all.

J: Perhaps rather with a process.

I: Or with what-is-the-case. But such terms will quickly land us in inadequacies.

J: But only if we already somehow have in view what our saying would want to reach.

I: It can hardly have escaped you that in my later writings I no longer employ the term "hermeneutics."

J: You are said to have changed your standpoint.

I: I have left an earlier standpoint, not in order to exchange it for another one, but because even the former standpoint was merely a way-station along a way. The lasting element in thinking is the way. And ways of thinking hold within them that mysterious quality that we can walk them forward and backward, and that indeed only the way back will lead us forward.

J: Obviously you do not mean "forward" in the sense of an advance, but . . . I have difficulty in finding the right word.

I: "Fore"—into that nearest nearness which we constantly rush ahead of, and which strikes us as strange each time anew when we catch sight of it.

J: And which we therefore quickly dismiss again from view, to stay instead with what is familiar and profitable.

I: While the nearness which we constantly overtake would rather bring us back.

J: Back—yes, but back where?

I: Into what is beginning.

J: I find this difficult to understand, if I am to think in terms of what you have said about it in your writings up to now.

I: Even so, you have already pointed to it, when you spoke of the presence that springs from the mutual calling of origin and future.

J: As you may have surmised, I see more clearly as soon as I think in terms of our Japanese experience. But I am not certain whether you have your eye on the same.

I: That could prove itself in our dialogue.

J: We Japanese do not think it strange if a dialogue leaves undefined what is really intended, or even restores it back to the keeping of the undefinable.

I: That is part, I believe, of every dialogue that has turned out well between thinking beings. As if of its own accord, it can take care that that undefinable something not only does not slip away, but displays its gathering force ever more luminously in the course of the dialogue.

J: Our dialogues with Count Kuki probably failed to turn out so well. We younger men challenged him much too directly to satisfy our thirst for handy information.

I: Thirst for knowledge and greed for explanations never lead to a thinking inquiry. Curiosity is always the concealed arrogance of a self-consciousness that banks on a self-invented *ratio* and its rationality. The *will* to know does not *will* to abide in hope before what is worthy of thought.

J: Thus we wanted to know in fact only how European aesthetics might be suitable to give a higher clarity to what endows our art and poetry with their nature.

I: And that would be?

J: We have for it the name I mentioned earlier: *Iki.*

I: How often did I hear that word on Kuki's lips, yet without experiencing what is said in it.

J: Meanwhile, what you mean to say with hermeneutics must somehow have illuminated *Iki* more brightly for Count Kuki.

I: I sensed as much, but never could follow him in his insights.

J: You have already mentioned what prevented you: the language of the dialogue was European; but what was to be experienced and to be thought was the Eastasian nature of Japanese art.

I: Whatever we spoke about was from the start forced over into the sphere of European ideas.

J: What made you aware of that?

I: The manner in which Kuki explained the basic word *Iki.* He spoke of sensuous radiance through whose lively delight there breaks the radiance of something suprasensuous.

J: With that explanation, I believe, Kuki has hit on what we experience in Japanese art.

I: Your experience, then, moves within the difference between a sensuous and a suprasensuous world. This is the distinction on which rests what has long been called Western metaphysics.

J: With this reference to the distinction that pervades metaphysics, you now touch the source of that danger of which we spoke. Our thinking, if I am allowed to call it that, does know something similar to the metaphysical distinction; but even so, the distinction itself and what it distinguishes cannot be comprehended with Western metaphysical concepts. We say *Iro,* that is, color, and say *Ku,* that is, emptiness, the open, the sky. We say: without *Iro,* no *Ku.*

I: This seems to correspond exactly to what Western, that is to say, metaphysical doctrine says about art when it represents art aesthetically. The *aistheton,* what can be perceived by the senses, lets the *noeton,* the nonsensuous, shine through.

J: Now you will understand how great the temptation was for Kuki to define *Iki* with the help of European aesthetics, that is, as you pointed out, define it metaphysically.

I: Even greater was and still is my fear that in this way the real nature of Eastasian art is obscured and shunted into a realm that is inappropriate to it.

J: I fully share your fear; for while *Iro* does indeed name color, it yet means essentially more than whatever is perceptible by the senses. *Ku* does indeed name emptiness and the open, and yet it means essentially more than that which is merely suprasensuous.

I: Your suggestions, which I can follow only from afar, increase my uneasiness. Even greater than the fear I mentioned is the expectation within me that our conversation, which has grown out of our memory of Count Kuki, could turn out well.

J: You mean it could bring us nearer to what is unsaid?

I: That alone would give us an abundance to think on.

J: Why do you say "would"?

I: Because I now see *still* more clearly the danger that the language of our dialogue might constantly destroy the possibility of saying that of which we are speaking.

J: Because this language itself rests on the metaphysical distinction between the sensuous and the suprasensuous, in that the structure of the language is supported by the basic elements of sound and script on the one hand, and signification and sense on the other.

I: At least within the purview of European ideas. Or is the situation the same with you?

J: Hardly. But, as I indicated, the temptation is great to rely on European ways of representation and their concepts.

I: That temptation is reinforced by a process which I would call the complete Europeanization of the earth and of man.

J: Many people consider this process the triumphal march of reason. At the end of the eighteenth century, in the French Revolution, was not reason proclaimed a goddess?

I: Indeed. The idolization of that divinity is in fact carried so far that any thinking which rejects the claim of reason as not originary, simply has to be maligned today as unreason.

J: The incontestable dominance of your European reason is thought to be confirmed by the successes of that rationality which technical advances set before us at every turn.

I: This delusion is growing, so that we are no longer able to see how the Europeanization of man and of the earth attacks at the source everything that is of an essential nature. It seems that these sources are to dry up.

J: A striking example for what you have in mind is the internationally known film *Rashomon*. Perhaps you have seen it.

I: Fortunately yes; unfortunately, only once. I believed that I was experiencing the enchantment of the Japanese world, the enchantment that carries us away into the mysterious. And so I do not understand why you offer just this film as an example of an all-consuming Europeanization.

J: We Japanese consider the presentation frequently too realistic, for example in the dueling scenes.

I: But are there not also subdued gestures?

J: Inconspicuities of this kind flow abundantly and hardly noticeable to a European observer. I recall a hand resting on another person, in which there is concentrated a contact that remains infinitely remote from any touch, something that may not even be called gesture any longer in the sense in which I understand your usage. For this hand is suffused and borne by a call calling from afar and calling still farther onward, because stillness has brought it.

I: But in view of such gestures, which differ from our gestures, I fail even more to understand how you can mention this film as an example of Europeanization.

J: Indeed it cannot be understood, because I am still expressing myself inadequately. And yet, for an adequate expression I need precisely your language.

I: And at this point you do not heed the danger?

J: Perhaps it can be banished for a few moments.

I: As long as you speak of realism, you are talking the language of metaphysics, and move within the distinction between the real as sensuous, and the ideal as nonsensuous.

J: You are right. However, with my reference to realism, I did not mean so much the massiveness of presentation which is scattered here and there throughout the film, and which remains unavoidable, in any event, in consideration of the *non*-Japanese audience.

Ultimately, I did mean something else altogether with my reference to realism in the film—this, that the Japanese world is captured and imprisoned at all in the objectness of photography, and is in fact especially framed for photography.

I: If I have listened rightly, you would say that the Eastasian world, and the technical-aesthetic product of the film industry, are incompatible.

J: This is what I have in mind. Regardless of what the aesthetic quality of a Japanese film may turn out to be, the mere fact that our world is set forth in the frame of a film forces that world into the sphere of what you call objectness. The photographic objectification is already a consequence of the ever wider outreach of Europeanization.

I: A European will find it difficult to understand what you mean.

J: Certainly, and especially because the foreground world of Japan is altogether European or, if you will, American. The background world of Japan, on the other hand, or better, that world itself, is what you experience in the *No* play.

I: I know only a book *about* the *No*-play.

J: Which, may I ask?

I: Benl's Academy treatise.

J: In Japan, it is considered an extremely thorough piece of work, and by far the best thing you can read on the *No*-play.

I: But reading alone is hardly enough.

J: You would need to attend such plays. But even that remains hard as long as you are unable to live within Japanese existence. To allow you to see, even if only from afar, something of what the *No*-play defines, I would assist you with one remark. You know that the Japanese stage is empty.

I: That emptiness demands uncommon concentration.

J: Thanks to that concentration, only a slight additional gesture on the actor's part is required to cause mighty things to appear out of a strange stillness.

I: How am I to understand you?

J: For instance, if a mountain landscape, is to appear, the actor slowly raises his open hand and holds it quietly above his eyes at eyebrow level. May I show you?

I: Please do.
   (The Japanese raises and holds his hand as described.)

I: That is indeed a gesture with which a European will hardly be content.

J: With it all, the gesture subsists less in the visible movement of the hand, nor primarily in the stance of the body. The essence of what your language calls "gesture" is hard to say.

I: And yet, the word "gesture" helps us experience truly what is here to be said.

J: Ultimately, it coincides with what I have in mind.

I: Gesture is the gathering of a bearing.

J: No doubt you intentionally avoid saying: *our* bearing.

I: Because what truly bears, only bears itself *toward* us . . .

J: . . . though we bear only our share to its encounter.

I: While that which bears itself toward us has already borne our counterbearing into the gift it bears for us.

J: Thus you call bearing or gesture: the gathering which originarily unites within itself what we bear to it and what it bears to us.

I: However, with this formulation we still run the risk that we understand the gathering as a subsequent union . . .

J: . . . instead of experiencing that all bearing, in giving and encounter, springs first and only from the gathering.

I: If we were to succeed in thinking of gesture in this sense, where would you then look for the essence of that gesture which you showed me?

J: In a beholding that is itself invisible, and that, so gathered, bears itself to encounter emptiness in such a way that in and through it the mountains appear.

I: That emptiness then is the same as nothingness, that essential being which we attempt to add in our thinking, as the other, to all that is present and absent.

J: Surely. For this reason we in Japan understood at once your lecture "What is Metaphysics?" when it became available to us in 1930 through a translation which a Japanese student, then attending your lectures, had ventured. —We marvel to this day how the Europeans could lapse into interpreting as nihilistic the nothingness of which you speak in that lecture. To us, emptiness is the loftiest name for what you mean to say with the word "Being" . . .

I: . . . in a thinking attempt whose first steps are unavoidable even to this day. It did, however, become the occasion for very great confusion, a confusion grounded in the matter itself and linked with the use of the name "Being." For this name belongs, after all, to the patrimony of the language of metaphysics, while I put that word into a title of an essay which brings out the essence of metaphysics, and only thus brings metaphysics back within its own limits.

J: When you speak of overcoming metaphysics, this is what you have in mind.

I: This only; neither a destruction nor even a denial of metaphysics. To intend anything else would be childish presumption and a demeaning of history.

J: To us, at a distance, it had always seemed amazing that people never tired of imputing to you a negative attitude toward the history of previous thinking, while in fact you strive only for an original appropriation.

I: Whose success can and should be disputed.

J: The fact that this dispute has not yet got onto the right track is owing—among many other motives—in the main to the confusion that your ambiguous use of the word "Being" has created.

I: You are right: only, the insidious thing is that the confusion which has been occasioned is afterward ascribed to my own thinking attempt, an attempt which on its own way knows with full clarity the difference between "Being" as "the Beings of beings," and "Being" as "Being" in respect of its proper sense, that is, in respect of its truth (the clearing).

J: Why did you not surrender the word "Being" immediately and resolutely to the exclusive use of the language of metaphysics? Why did you not at once give its own name to what you were searching for, by way of the nature of Time, as the "sense of Being"?

I: How is one to give a name to what he is still searching for? To assign the naming word is, after all, what constitutes finding.

J: Then the confusion that has arisen must be endured.

I: Indeed, perhaps for long, and perhaps only in this way, that we painstakingly labor to unravel it.

J: Only this will lead us out into the open.

I: But the way there cannot be staked out according to a plan, like a road. Thinking is fond of a manner of road-building that is, I would almost say, wondrous.

J: A manner in which the builders must at times return to construction sites they left behind, or go back even further.

I: I am amazed by your insight into the nature of the paths of thinking.

J: We have rich experience in the matter; only it has not been reduced to the form of a conceptual methodology, which destroys every moving force of the thinking steps. Besides, you yourself have caused me to see the path of your thinking more clearly.

I: How?

J: Lately, even though you employ the word "Being" sparingly, you yet have used the name once again in a context which does in fact come home to me more and more closely as what is most essential in your thinking. In your "Letter on Humanism" you characterize language as the "house of Being"; today, at the beginning of our dialogue, you referred to this phrase yourself. And while I am recalling it, I must consider that our dialogue has strayed far from its path.

I: So it appears. In truth, however, we are only about to get onto that path.

J: At the moment, I do not see it. We were trying to speak about Kuki's aesthetic interpretation of *Iki.*

I: We were trying, and in the process could not avoid considering the danger of such dialogues.

J: We recognized that the danger lies in the concealed nature of language.

I: And just now you mentioned the phrase "house of Being," which would suggest the essence of language.

J: Thus we have indeed stayed on the path of the dialogue.

I: Probably only because we, without quite knowing it, were obedient to what alone, according to your words, allows a dialogue to succeed.

J: It is that undefined defining something . . .

I: . . . which we leave in unimpaired possession of the voice of its promptings.

J: At the risk that this voice, in our case, is silence itself.

I: What are you thinking of now?

J: Of the Same as you have in mind, of the nature of language.

I: That is what is defining our dialogue. But even so we must not touch it.

J: Surely not, if by touching you mean grasping it in the sense of your European conceptualizations.

I: No, those conceptualizations are not what I have in mind. Even the phrase "house of Being" does not provide a concept of the nature of language, to the great sorrow of the philosophers who in their disgruntlement see in such phrases no more than a decay of thinking.

J: I, too, find much food for thought in your phrase "house of Being"—but on different grounds. I feel that it touches upon the nature of language without doing it injury. For if it is necessary to leave the defining something in full possession of its voice, this does in no way mean that our thinking should not pursue the nature of language. Only the manner in which the attempt is made is decisive.

I: And so I now take courage to ask a question which has long troubled me, and which your visit now almost compels me to ask.

J: Do not count too heavily on my powers to follow your questions. Our dialogue, meanwhile, has anyhow made me much more aware of how un-thought everything still is that concerns the nature of language.

I: And especially since the nature of language remains something altogether different for the Eastasian and the European peoples.

J: And what you call "nature" also remains different. How, then, could our reflection get out into the open?

I: Most easily if from the very outset we do not demand too much. Thus I shall permit myself for the moment to put to you an altogether preliminary question.

J: I fear that even this question can hardly be answered unless we disregard the danger of our dialogue.

I: That cannot be, since we are walking toward the danger.

J: Then ask away.

I: What does the Japanese world understand by language? Asked still more cautiously: Do you have in your language a word for what we call language? If not, how do you experience what with us is called language?

J: No one has ever asked me that question. And it seems to me also that we in our own Japanese world pay no heed to what you are asking me now. I must beg you, then, to allow me a few moments of reflection.
(*The Japanese closes his eyes, lowers his head, and sinks into a long reflection. The Inquirer waits until his guest resumes the conversation.*)

J: There is a Japanese word that says the essential being of language, rather than being of use as a name for speaking and for language.

I: The matter itself requires that, because the essential *being* of language cannot be anything linguistic. The same holds true for the phrase "house of Being."

J: From a great distance I sense a kinship between our word that is now before my mind, and your phrase.

I: The phrase gives a hint of the nature of language.

J: It seems to me you have just said a freeing word.

I: Then that hint would be the word's basic character.

J: Only now that you speak of hint, a word I could not find, something becomes clearer to me that I had merely surmised when I read your "Letter on Humanism," and translated into Japanese your lecture on Hölderlin's elegy "Home-coming." During the same period I was translating Kleist's *Penthesilea* and the *Amphitryon.*

I: The nature of the German language must at that time have come over you like a waterfall.

J: It did indeed. And while I was translating, I often felt as though I were wandering back and forth between two differ-ent language realities, such that at moments a radiance shone on me which let me sense that the wellspring of reality from which those two fundamentally different lan-guages arise was the same.

I: You did not, then, seek for a general concept under which both the European and the Eastasian languages could be subsumed.

J: Absolutely not. When you now speak of hints, this freeing word emboldens me to name to you the word by which to us the nature of language is—how shall I say . . .

I: . . . perhaps hinted.

J: That is to the point. But even so I fear that to call your "house of Being" a hint might tempt you and me to elaborate the notion of hinting into a guiding concept in which we then bundle up everything.

I: That must not happen.

J: How will you prevent it?

I: It can never be prevented in the sense of being totally excluded.

J: Why not?

I: Because the mode of conceptual representation insinuates itself all too easily into every kind of human experience.

J: Even where thinking is in a certain sense concept-less?

I: Even there—you need only recall how instantly you accepted Kuki's aesthetic interpretation of *Iki* as appropriate, even though it rests on European, that is to say, on metaphysical ideas.

J: If I understand you rightly, you mean to say that the metaphysical manner of forming ideas is in a certain respect unavoidable.

I: That is what Kant saw clearly, in his own way.

J: Yet we realize only rarely the full implications of his insight.

I: Because Kant was unable to develop it beyond metaphysics. The unbroken rule of metaphysics establishes itself even where we do not expect it—in the elaboration of logic into logistics.

J: Do you consider that a metaphysical process?

I: Indeed I do. And the attack upon the nature of language which is concealed in that process, perhaps the last attack from that quarter, remains unheeded.

J: We must guard all the more carefully the ways toward the nature or reality of language.

I: It would even be enough if we were to succeed only in building a bypath toward those ways.

J: Your speaking of hints seems to me to indicate a trail that might lead to such a path.

I: But even to talk of a hint is to venture too much.

J: We understand only too well that a thinker would prefer to hold back the word that is to be said, not in order to keep it for himself, but to bear it toward his encounter with what is to be thought.

I: That is in keeping with the hints. They are enigmatic. They beckon to us. They beckon *away.* They beckon us *toward* that from which they unexpectedly bear themselves toward us.

J: You are thinking of hints as belonging together with what you have explained by the word "gesture" or "bearing."

I: That is so.

J: Hints and gestures, according to what you indicated, differ from signs and chiffres, all of which have their habitat in metaphysics.

I: Hints and gestures belong to an entirely different realm of reality, if you will allow this term which seems treacherous even to myself.

J: What you suggest confirms a surmise I have long cherished. Your phrase "house of Being" must not be taken as a mere hasty image which helps us in imagining what we will, such as: house is a shelter erected earlier somewhere or other, in which Being, like a portable object, can be stored away.

I: That notion proves invalid as soon as we think of the ambiguity of "Being" of which we have spoken. With that expression, I do not mean the Being of beings represented metaphysically, but the presence of Being, more precisely the presence of the two-fold, Being and beings—but this two-fold understood in respect of its importance for thinking them.

J: If we heed this, then your phrase can never become a mere catchword.

I: It already has become one.

J: Because you demand too much of today's manner of thinking.

I: Too much, quite true, too much of what has not yet ripened.

J: You mean ripened so that it drops like a fruit from a tree. It seems to me that there are no such words. A saying that would wait *for that* would not be in keeping with the nature of language. And you yourself are the last person who would lay claim to such saying.

I: You do me too much honor. May I return the honor by surmising that you are nearer to the reality of language than all our concepts.

J: Not I, but the word for which you are asking, the word which I, now somewhat emboldened, may hardly withhold from you any longer.

I: This remark tells me that your word, still withheld, for the reality of what we call language will bring us a surprise such as we dare not hope for even now.

J: That could be. That surprise, however—which will strike you with the same force with which it is holding me captive ever since your question—needs to have the possibility of swinging widely.

I: Which is why you hesitate.

J: Emboldened by your indication that the word is a hint, and not a sign in the sense of mere signification.

I: Hints need the widest sphere in which to swing . . .

J: . . . where mortals go to and fro only slowly.

I: This is what our language calls "hesitate." It is done truly when slowness rests on shy reverence. And so I do not wish to disturb your hesitation by urging you on too rashly.

J: You are more helpful to me in my attempt to say the word than you can know.

I: I shall not hide from you that you are throwing me into a state of great agitation, especially because all my efforts to get an answer to my question from language experts and linguistic scholars of language have so far been in vain. But in order that your reflection may swing freely, almost without your prompting, let us exchange roles, and let me be the one who gives the answers, specifically the answer to your question about hermeneutics.

J: We are back, then, on the path which we took first in our dialogue.

I: A path on which we did not get very far with an explication of hermeneutics. I told you stories, rather, showing how I came to employ the word.

J: While I, in turn, noted that now you do not use it any longer.

I: Finally, I emphasized that hermeneutics, used as an adjunct word to "phenomenology," does not have its usual meaning, methodology of interpretation, but means the interpretation itself.

J: Then our dialogue drifted away into the undefined.

I: Fortunately.

J: Even so, I thank you for coming back once more to hermeneutics.

I: As I do so, I would like to start from the etymology of the word; it will show you that my use of the word is not arbitrary, and that it also is apt to clarify the intention of my experiment with phenomenology.

J: I am all the more puzzled that you have meanwhile dropped both words.

I: That was done, not—as is often thought—in order to deny the significance of phenomenology, but in order to abandon my own path of thinking to namelessness.

J: An effort with which you will hardly be successful . . .

I: . . . since one cannot get by in public without rubrics.

J: But that cannot prevent you from giving also a more precise explanation of the terms "hermeneutics" and "hermeneutic" which you have meanwhile abandoned.

I: I shall be glad to try, because the explanation may issue in a discussion.

J: In the sense in which your lecture on Trakl's poetry* understands discussion.

I: Exactly in that sense. The expression "hermeneutic" derives from the Greek verb *hermeneuein.* That verb is related to the noun *hermeneus,* which is referable to the name of the god Hermes by a playful thinking that is more compelling than the rigor of science. Hermes is the divine messenger. He brings the message of destiny; *hermeneuein* is that exposition which brings tidings because it can listen to a message. Such exposition becomes an interpretation of what has been said earlier by the poets who, according to Socrates in Plato's *Ion* (534e), *hermenes eisin ton theon*—"are interpreters of the gods."

J: I am very fond of this short Platonic dialogue. In the passage you have in mind, Socrates carries the affinities even further by surmising that the rhapsodes are those who bear the tidings of the poets' word.

I: All this makes it clear that hermeneutics means not just the interpretation but, even before it, the bearing of message and tidings.

*See below, p. 159. (Ed.)

J: Why do you stress this original sense of *hermeneuein?*

I: Because it was this original sense which prompted me to use it in defining the phenomenological thinking that opened the way to *Being and Time* for me. What mattered then, and still does, is to bring out the Being of beings—though no longer in the manner of metaphysics, but such that Being itself will shine out, Being itself—that is to say: the presence of present beings, the two-fold of the two in virtue of their simple oneness. This is what makes its claim on man, calling him to its essential being.

J: Man, then, realizes his nature as man by corresponding to the call of the two-fold, and bears witness to it in its message.

I: Accordingly, what prevails in and bears up the relation of human nature to the two-fold is language. Language defines the hermeneutic relation.

J: Thus when I ask you about hermeneutics, and when you ask me what our word is for what you call language, we ask each other the Same.

I: Clearly, and that is why we may confidently entrust ourselves to the hidden drift of our dialogue . . .

J: . . . as long as we remain inquirers.

I: You do not mean that we are pumping each other, out of curiosity, but . . .

J: . . . but rather that we go right on releasing into the open whatever might be said.

I: That could all too easily give the impression that everything we say drifts away noncommittally.

J: We can counter that impression by paying heed to the doctrines of past thinkers, and always let them, too, take part in our dialogue. What I have just said is something I learned from you.

I: What you learned there has been learned in turn by listening to the thinkers' thinking. <u>Each man is in each instance in dialogue with his forebears, and perhaps even more and in a more hidden manner with those who will come after him.</u>

J: In a deeper sense, this historical nature of every thinking dialogue is not, however, in need of all those enterprises which, in the manner of historiography, report things from the past about the thinkers and what they have thought.

I: Certainly not. But for us today it may become a pressing need to prepare such conversations, by interpreting properly what earlier thinkers have said.

J: Something that could easily degenerate into mere busywork.

I: That is a danger we stave off as long as we ourselves make an effort to think in dialogue.

J: And, as you say in your language, weigh each word.

I: But, above all, examine whether each word in each case is given its full—most often hidden—weight.

J: It seems to me that we are following this unwritten prescription, though I must confess that I am a very clumsy questioner.

I: All of us remain clumsy questioners. Despite much care, we still keep overlooking essentials—even here, in this dialogue, which led us to discuss hermeneutics and the reality of language.

J: For the moment I fail to see in what way we were careless in our use of words.

I: That is something we often notice only quite late, because the fault lies not so much in ourselves as in the fact that language is more powerful than we, and therefore weightier.

J: In what sense?

I: To illustrate by what we were just talking of . . .

J: You said that language is the fundamental trait in human nature's hermeneutic relation to the two-fold of presence and present beings. To that remark I at once intended to make a few observations; but I shall do so only after you have shown just what we have failed to think of in that context.

I: I mean the word "relation." We think of it in the sense of a relationship. What we know in that way we can identify in an empty, formal sense, and employ like a mathematical notation. Think of the procedure of logistics. But in the phrase, "man stands in hermeneutical relation to the two-fold," we may hear the word "relation" also in a wholly different way. In fact, we must, if we give thought to what was said. Presumably, we must and can do so not right away but in good time, after long reflection.

J: Then it will do no harm if for the time being we understand "relation" in the customary sense of relationship.

I: True—but it is inadequate from the start, assuming that this word "relation" is to become a mainstay of our statement.

We say "correlation" also when talking about the supply and demand of commodities. If man is in a hermeneutical relation, however, that means that he is precisely *not* a commodity. But the word "relation" does want to say that man, in his very being, is in demand, is needed, that he, as the being he is, belongs within a needfulness which claims him.

J: In what sense?

I: Hermeneutically—that is to say, with respect to bringing tidings, with respect to preserving a message.

J: Man stands "in relation" then says the same as: Man *is* really as man when needed and used by . . .

I: . . . what calls on man to preserve the two-fold . . .

J: . . . which, as far as I can see, cannot be explained in terms of presence, nor in terms of present beings, nor in terms of the relation of the two.

I: Because it is only the two-fold itself which unfolds the clarity, that is, the clearing in which present beings as such, and presence, can be discerned by man . . .

J: . . . by man who by nature stands in relation to, that is, is being used by, the two-fold.

I: This is also why we may no longer say: relation to the two-fold, for the two-fold is not an object of mental representation, but is the sway of usage.

J: Which we never experience directly, however, as long as we think of the two-fold only as the difference which becomes apparent in a comparison that tries to contrast present beings and their presence.

I: I am surprised that you see so clearly.

J: When I can follow you in the dialogue, I succeed. Left *alone,* I am helpless; for even the manner in which you employ the words "relation" and "use" . . .

I: . . . or, better, the manner in which I *use* them . . .

J: . . . is strange enough.

I: I don't deny it. But it seems to me that, in the field in which we are moving, we reach those things with which we are originally familiar precisely if we do not shun passing through things strange to us.

J: In what sense do you understand "originarily familiar"? You do not mean what we know first, do you?

I: No—but what before all else has been entrusted to our nature, and becomes known only at the last.

J: And that is what your thinking pursues.

I: Only that—but in this way, that in it there is veiled all that is worthy of thought as such and as a whole.

J: And in that thinking, you pay no heed to the current ideas of your fellows.

I: It seems that way, of course; but in truth, every thinking step only serves the effort to help man in his thinking to find the path of his essential being.

J: Hence your reflection on language . . .

I: . . . on language in its relation to the nature of Being, that is to say, to the sway of the two-fold.

J: But if language is the basic trait in hermeneutically defined usage, then you experience the reality of language from the start differently from the way one does in metaphysical thinking. This is what I had intended to point out earlier.

I: But what for?

J: Not for the sake of contrasting something new with the conventional, but to remind us that our dialogue speaks historically precisely in its attempt to reflect on the nature of language.

I: It speaks out of a thinking respect of the past.

J: And this is just what was to be noted in the title of the lecture series the copy of which was frequently discussed in the twenties among us Japanese.

I: I must be frank and tell you that here you are mistaken. The lecture series "Expression and Appearance" (or was not the title "Expression and Meaning"?) was still rather controversial, even though it remained informed by what we now call the historic character of thinking dialogue.

J: The title, then, was to point up a contrast.

I: In any event, I was concerned to bring into view that which is wholly different—of which, however, I had only an obscure if not confused intimation. Such youthful capers easily lead to doing injustice.

J: The word "expression" in the title is the name for what you oppose. For your gaze into the nature of language does not fasten upon the phonetics and the written forms of the words, which are generally conceived to constitute the expressive character of language.

I: The name "expression" is here understood in the narrow sense of sensuous appearance. Yet even where our attention is focused on the content of meaning in the phonetic and written formations, even there language is still conceived as expressive in character.

J: How so? Speech understood in the fullness of its meaning transcends—and does so always—the physical-sensible side of phonetics. Language, as sense that is sounded and written, is in itself suprasensuous, something that constantly transcends the merely sensible. So understood, language is in itself metaphysical.

I: I agree with everything you propose. But language makes its appearance in this metaphysical nature only insofar as it is beforehand understood to be expression. Expression does not mean here only the enunciated sounds of speech and the printed signs of writing. Expression is simultaneously utterance.

J: Utterance refers to its inwardness, to what pertains to the soul.

I: In the days of that lecture, everyone was talking about experience (*Erlebnis*), even within phenomenology.

J: A famous book by Dilthey has the title *Experience and Poetry.*

I: To experience in this sense always means to refer back—to refer life and lived experience back to the "I." Experience is the name for the referral of the objective back to the subject. The much-discussed I/Thou experience, too, belongs within the metaphysical sphere of subjectivity.

J: And this sphere of subjectivity and of the expression that belongs to it is what you left behind when you entered into the hermeneutic relation to the two-fold.

I: At least I tried. The guiding notions which, under the names "expression," "experience," and "consciousness," determine modern thinking, were to be put in question with respect to the decisive role they played.

J: But then I no longer understand how you could choose the title "Expression and Appearance." It was intended, was it not, to announce a contrast. "Expression" is the utterance of something internal and refers to the subjective. "Appearance," on the contrary, names the objective, if I may here recall Kant's usage according to which appearances are the objects, the objects of experience. By giving your lecture that title, you did commit yourself to the subject-object relation.

I: In a certain respect your objection is justified, if only for the reason that much had to remain unclear in those lectures. Nobody can in just one single leap take distance from the predominant circle of ideas, especially not if he is dealing with the well-worn tracks of traditional thinking—tracks that fade into realms where they can hardly be seen. Besides, taking such distance from all tradition is tempered by the very fact that the seemingly subversive will tries above all to recover the things of the past in a more originary form. It is on purpose that the first page of *Being and Time* speaks of "raising again" a question. What is meant is not the monotonous trotting out of something that is always the same, but: to fetch, to gather in, to bring together what is concealed within the old.

J: Our teachers and my friends in Japan have always understood your efforts in that sense. Professor Tanabe often came back to a question you once put to him: why it was that we Japanese did not call back to mind the venerable beginnings of our own thinking, instead of chasing ever more greedily after the latest news in European philosophy. As a matter of fact, we do so still today.

I: It is not easy to go counter to that tendency. Such procedures, in good time, are smothered by their own sterility. But what requires our contribution is a different matter.

J: Which would be?

I: To give heed to the trails that direct thinking back into the region of its source.

J: Do you find such trails in your own attempt?

I: I *find* them only because they are *not* of my own making, and are discernible only quite rarely, like the wind-borne echo of a distant call.

J: But I would gather then that in the distinction "Expression and Appearance," you are no longer basing yourself on the subject-object relation.

I: You will see it even more clearly if you attend to what I would now like to add to your mention of Kant's concept of appearance. Kant's definition is based on the event that everything present has already become the object of our representation.

J: In appearance as Kant thinks of it, our experience must already include the object as something in opposition to us.

I: That is necessary not only in order to understand Kant properly, but also and above all else so that we may experience the appearing of the appearance, if I may put it that way, originarily.

J: How does this happen?

I: The Greeks were the first to experience and think of *phainomena* as phenomena. But in that experience it is thoroughly alien to the Greeks to press present beings into an opposing objectness; *phainesthai* means to them that a being assumes its radiance, and in that radiance it appears. Thus appearance is still the basic trait of the presence of all present beings, as they rise into unconcealment.

J: Accordingly, in your title "Expression and Appearance" you use the second noun in the Greek sense?

I: Yes and no. Yes, in that for me the name "appearance" does not name objects as objects, and least of all as objects of consciousness—consciousness always meaning self-consciousness.

J: In short: appearance *not* in the Kantian sense.

I: Merely to contrast it with Kant is not enough. For even where the term "object" is used for present beings as subsisting within themselves, and Kant's interpretation of objectness is rejected, we are still far from thinking of appearance in the Greek sense—but fundamentally though rather in a very hidden sense, in the manner of Descartes: in terms of the "I" as the subject.

J: Yet your "no" suggests that you, too, do not think of appearance in the Greek sense.

I: You are right. What is decisive here is difficult to render visible, because it calls for simple and free vision.

J: Such vision, obviously, is still rare. For usually your definition of appearance is equated, sight unseen, with that of the Greeks; and it is considered a foregone conclusion that your thinking has no other aim than a return to Greek and even pre-Socratic thinking.

I: That opinion is foolish, of course, and yet it has something in mind that is correct.

J: How so?

I: To answer your question with the necessary brevity, I would venture a turn of phrase which is at once open to new misinterpretations . . .

J: . . . which you, however, can counter just as quickly.

I: Certainly, if it did not cause further delays in our dialogue, whose time is limited because tomorrow you will leave again, to go to Florence.

J: I have already decided to stay for another day, if you will allow me to visit you again.

I: There is nothing I would rather do. But even with this pleasant prospect I must keep the answer short.

J: How is it then with your relation to the thinking of the Greeks?

I: Our thinking today is charged with the task to think what the Greeks have thought in an even more Greek manner.

J: And so to understand the Greeks better than they have understood themselves.

I: No, that is not it; for all great thinking always understands itself best of all, that is to say, *itself* within the limits set for it.

J: Then, what does it mean: to think what the Greeks have thought in an even more Greek manner?

I: It can be readily explained with a view to the essence of appearance. If to be present itself is thought of as appearance, then there prevails in being present the emergence into openness in the sense of unconcealedness. This unconcealedness comes about in the unconcealment as a clearing; but this clearing itself, as occurrence, remains unthought in every respect. To enter into thinking this unthought occurrence means: to pursue more originally what the Greeks have thought, to see it in the source of its reality. To see it so is in its own way Greek, and yet in respect of what it sees is no longer, is never again, Greek.

J: Then, what is it?

I: It seems to me no answer to this question is incumbent on us. Nor would an answer help us, because what matters is to see appearance as the reality of presence in its essential origin.

J: If you succeed with that, then you are thinking of appearance in the Greek way, and at the same time no longer in the Greek way. You said—at least this was the sense of what you said—that we leave the sphere of the subject-object relation behind us when thinking enters into the experience just mentioned, in which the real origin of appearance— dare we say—itself appears?

I: Hardly. But you are touching on something essential. For in the source of appearance, something comes toward man that holds the two-fold of presence and present beings.

J: That two-fold has always already offered itself to man, although its nature remained veiled.

I: Man, to the extent he is man, listens to this message.

J: And that happens even while man gives no particular attention to the fact that he is ever listening already to that message.

I: Man is used for hearing the message.

J: This you called a while ago: man stands in a relation.

I: And the relation is called hermeneutical because it brings the tidings of that message.

J: This message makes the claim on man that he respond to it . . .

I: . . . to listen and belong to it as man.

J: And this is what you call *being* human, if you here still admit the word "being."

I: Man is the message-bearer of the message which the two-fold's unconcealment speaks to him.

J: As far as I am able to follow what you are saying, I sense a deeply concealed kinship with our thinking, precisely because your path of thinking and its language are so wholly other.

I: Your admission agitates me in a way which I can control only because we remain in dialogue. But there is one question I cannot leave out.

J: Which?

I: The question of the site in which the kinship that you sense comes into play.

J: Your question reaches far.

I: How so?

J: The distance is the boundlessness which is shown to us in *Ku,* which means the sky's emptiness.

I: Then, man, as the message-bearer of the message of the two-fold's unconcealment, would also be he who walks the boundary of the boundless.

J: And on this path he seeks the boundary's mystery . . .

I: . . . which cannot be hidden in anything other than the voice that determines and tunes his nature.

J: What we are now saying—forgive the "we"—can no longer be discussed on the strength of the metaphysical notion of language. Presumably this is why you tried to suggest that you were turning away from that notion by giving your lecture course the title "Expression and Appearance."

I: The entire course remained a suggestion. I never did more than follow a faint trail, but follow it I did. The trail was an almost imperceptible promise announcing that we would be set free into the open, now dark and perplexing, now again lightning-sharp like a sudden insight, which then, in turn, eluded every effort to say it.

J: Later, too, in *Being and Time,* your discussion of language remains quite sparse.

I: Even so, after our dialogue you may want to read Section 34 in *Being and Time* more closely.

J: I have read it many times, and each time regretted that you kept it so short. But I believe that now I see more clearly the full import of the fact that hermeneutics and language belong together.

I: The full import in what direction?

J: Toward a transformation of thinking—a transformation which, however, cannot be established as readily as a ship can alter its course, and even less can be established as the consequence of an accumulation of the results of philosophical research.

I: The transformation occurs as a passage . . .

J: . . . in which one site is left behind in favor of another . . .

I: . . . and that requires that the sites be placed in discussion.

J: One site is metaphysics.

I: And the other? We leave it without a name.

J: Meanwhile, I find it more and more puzzling how Count Kuki could get the idea that he could expect your path of thinking to be of help to him in his attempts in aesthetics, since your path, in leaving behind metaphysics, also leaves behind the aesthetics that is grounded in metaphysics.

I: But leaves it behind in such a way that we can only now give thought to the nature of aesthetics, and direct it back within its boundaries.

J: Perhaps it was this prospect that attracted Kuki; for he was much too sensitive, and much too thoughtful, to concern himself with the calculus of mere doctrines.

I: He used the European rubric "aesthetics," but what he thought and searched for was something else . . .

J: *Iki*—a word I dare not translate even now.

I: But perhaps you are now in a better position to describe the veiled hint that the word gives us.

J: Only after you have clarified the nature of the aesthetic.

I: That has already been done in the course of our dialogue —precisely where we did not specifically speak of it.

J: You mean when we discussed the subject-object relation?

I: Where else? Aesthetics, or shall we say, experience within the sphere in which it sets the standard, from the very start turns the art work into an object for our feelings and ideas. Only when the art work has become an object, only then is it fit for exhibitions and museums . . .

J: . . . and fit also to be valued and appraised.

I: Artistic quality becomes a distinguishing factor in contemporary-modern art experience.

J: Or shall we say straight out: in the art business.

I: But what is artistic is defined with reference to creativity and virtuosity.

J: Does art subsist in the artistic, or is it the other way around? All talk about the artistic seems to reveal that precedence is given to the artist . . .

I: . . . as the subject who remains related to the work as his object.

J: But this is the framework in which all aesthetics belongs.

I: That framework is so treacherous, that is to say, so all-embracing, that it can capture also all other kinds of experience of art and its nature.

J: It can embrace, but never make its own. This is why I fear now more than ever that every explication of *Iki* will fall into the clutches of aesthetic ideation.

I: It would depend—will you try?

J: *Iki* is the gracious.

I: As soon as you say this, we are at once in the midst of aesthetics—think of Schiller's treatise on "Grace and Dignity." That treatise, just as his later *Letters on the Aesthetic Education of Man,* was inspired by his dialogue with Kant's aesthetics.

J: If I am rightly informed, both works contributed a decisive stimulus for Hegel's *Aesthetics.*

I: And so it would be presumptuous if we now tried to convince ourselves with a few remarks that we have mastered the nature of aesthetics.

J: But speaking only by and large, I may attempt to detach *Iki,* which we just translated with "grace," from aesthetics, that is to say, from the subject-object relation. I do not now mean *gracious* in the sense of a stimulus that enchants . . .

I: . . . that is, not in the realm of what stimulates, of impressions, of *aisthesis*—but?

J: Rather in the opposite direction; but I am aware that with this indication I still remain embroiled in the realm of aesthetics.

I: If we keep this reservation in mind, there is no harm in your trying to give the explication just the same.

J: *Iki* is the breath of the stillness of luminous delight.

I: You understand "delight" literally, then, as what ensnares, carries away—into stillness.

J: There is in it nothing anywhere of stimulus and impression.

I: The delight is of the same kind as the hint that beckons on, and beckons to and fro.

J: The hint, however, is the message of the veiling that opens up.

I: Then, all presence would have its source in grace, in the sense of the pure delight of the beckoning stillness.

J: The fact that you give ear to me, or better, to the probing intimations I propose, awakens in me the confidence to drop my hesitations which have so far kept me from answering your question.

I: You mean the question which word in your language speaks for what we Europeans call "language."

J: Up to this moment I have shied away from that word, because I must give a translation which makes our word for language look like a mere pictograph, to wit, something that belongs within the precincts of conceptual ideas; for European science and its philosophy try to grasp the nature of language only by way of concepts.

I: What is the Japanese word for "language"?

J: (after further hesitation) It is *"Koto ba."*

I: And what does that say?

J: ba means leaves, including and especially the leaves of a blossom—petals. Think of cherry blossoms or plum blossoms.

I: And what does *Koto* say?

J: This is the question most difficult to answer. But it is easier now to attempt an answer because we have ventured to explain *Iki*: the pure delight of the beckoning stillness. The breath of stillness that makes this beckoning delight come into its own is the reign under which that delight is made to come. But *Koto* always also names that which in the event gives delight, itself, that which uniquely in each unrepeatable moment comes to radiance in the fullness of its grace.

I: Koto, then, would be the appropriating occurrence of the lightening message of grace.

J: Beautifully said! Only the word "grace" easily misleads the modern mind . . .

I: . . . leads it away into the precincts of impressions . . .

J: . . . whose corollary is always expression as the manner in which something is set free. It seems to me more helpful to turn to the Greek word *charis,* which I found in the lovely saying that you quote from Sophocles, in your lecture " . . . Poetically Man Dwells . . .", and translated "graciousness." This saying comes closer to putting into words the breathlike advent of the stillness of delight.

I: And something else, too, that I wanted to say there but could not offer within the context of the lecture. *charis* is there called *tiktousa*—that which brings forward and forth. Our German word *dichten, tihton* says the same. Thus Sophocles' lines portend to us that graciousness is itself poetical, is itself what really makes poetry, the welling-up of the message of the two-fold's unconcealment.

J: I would need more time than our dialogue allows to follow in thought the new prospects you have opened with your remark. But *one* thing I see at once—that your remark helps me to say more clearly what *Koto* is.

I: And that seems to me indispensable if I am to think at all adequately your Japanese word for "language," *Koto ba,* along with you.

J: You well remember that point in our dialogue where I named to you the Japanese words allegedly corresponding to the distinction between *aistheton* and *noeton*: *Iro* and *Ku.* *Iro* means more than color and whatever can be perceived by the senses. *Ku,* the open, the sky's emptiness, means more than the supra-sensible.

I: You could not say in what the "more" consists.

J: But now I can follow a hint which the two words hold.

I: In what direction do they hint?

J: Toward the source from which the mutual interplay of the two comes to pass.

I: Which is?

J: *Koto,* the happening of the lightening message of the graciousness that brings forth.

I: *Koto* would be the happening holding sway . . .

J: . . . holding sway over that which needs the shelter of all that flourishes and flowers.

I: Then, as the name for language, what does *Koto ba* say?

J: Language, heard through this word, is: the petals that stem from *Koto.*

I: That is a wondrous word, and therefore inexhaustible to our thinking. It names something other than our names, understood metaphysically, present to us: language, *glossa, lingua, langue.* For long now, I have been loth to use the word "language" when thinking on its nature.

J: But can you find a more fitting word?

I: I believe I have found it; but I would guard it against being used as a current tag, and corrupted to signify a concept.

J: Which word do you use?

I: The word "Saying." It means: saying and what is said in it and what is to be said.

J: What does "say" mean?

I: Probably the same as "show" in the sense of: let appear and let shine, but in the manner of hinting.

J: Saying, then, is not the name for human speaking . . .

I: . . . but for that essential being which your Japanese word *Koto ba* hints and beckons: that which is like a saga . . .

J: . . . and in whose beckoning hint I have come to be at home only now through our dialogue, so that now I also see more clearly how well-advised Count Kuki was when he, under your guidance, tried to reflect his way through hermeneutics.

I: But you also see how meager my guidance was bound to be; for the thinking look into the nature of Saying is only the beginning of that path which takes us back out of merely metaphysical representations, to where we heed the hints of that message whose proper bearers we would want to become.

J: That path is long.

I: Not so much because it leads far away, but because it leads through what is near.

J: Which is as near, and has long been as near, as the word for the reality of language, *Koto ba*—a word to which so far no thought has been given—is to us Japanese.

I: Petals that stem from *Koto*. Imagination would like to roam away into still unexperienced realms when this word begins its saying.

J: It could roam only if it were let go into mere representational ideas. But where imagination wells up as the wellspring of thinking, it seems to me to gather rather than to stray. Kant already had an intimation of something of the sort, as you yourself have shown.

I: But *is* our thinking already at that wellspring?

J: If not, then it is on its way there as soon as it seeks the path to which—as I now see more clearly—our Japanese word for language might beckon.

I: In order that we may yield to that hint, we would have to be more experienced in the nature of language.

J: It seems to me that efforts in that direction have accompanied your path of thinking for decades—and in so many forms that you are by now sufficiently prepared to say something about the nature of language as Saying.

I: But you know equally well that one's own effort alone is never adequate.

J: That remains true. But what mortal strength by itself cannot accomplish, we can attain more readily if we are full ready to give away freely whatever it may be that we attempt on our own, even if it falls short of perfection.

I: I have ventured some provisional remarks in the lecture which I gave several times in recent years, entitled "Language."*

J: I have read reports and even a transcript of that lecture.

I: Such transcripts, even if made carefully, remain dubious sources—as I said earlier—and any transcript of that lecture is, anyway, a distortion of its saying.

J: What do you mean by this harsh judgment?

I: It is a judgment not about transcripts, but about an unclear characterization of the lecture.

J: How so?

I: The lecture is not speaking *about* language . . .

J: But?

I: If I could answer you now, the darkness surrounding the path would be lighted. But I cannot answer—on the same grounds that have so far kept me from letting the lecture appear in print.

J: It would be forward of me to ask what those grounds are. After the way in which you a moment ago listened and took in our Japanese word for language, and from what you suggested about the message of the two-fold's unconcealment, and about man the message-bearer, I can only surmise vaguely what it means to transform the question of language into a reflection on the nature of Saying.

I: You will forgive me if I am still sparing with indications that could perhaps lead to a discussion of the nature of Saying.

J: That would call for a journey into the region where the essential being of Saying is at home.

---

*In Martin Heidegger, *Poetry, Language, and Thought* (tr. A. Hofstadter; New York: Harper & Row, 1971).

I: That before all else. But for the moment I have something else in mind. What prompts my reserve is the growing insight into the untouchable which is veiled from us by the mystery of Saying. A mere clarification of the difference between saying and speaking would gain us little.

J: We Japanese have—I think I may say so—an innate understanding for your kind of reserve. A mystery is a mystery only when it does not even come out *that* mystery is at work.

I: To those who are superficial and in a hurry, no less than to those who are deliberate and reflective, it must look as though there were no mystery anywhere.

J: But we are surrounded by the danger, not just of talking too loudly about the mystery, but of missing its working.

I: To guard the purity of the mystery's wellspring seems to me hardest of all.

J: But does that give us the right simply to shun the trouble and the risk of speaking about language?

I: Indeed not. We must incessantly strive for such speaking. What is so spoken cannot, of course, take the form of a scientific dissertation . . .

J: . . . because the movement of the questioning that is called for here might too easily congeal.

I: That would be the smallest loss. Something else is more weighty, and that is, whether there ever is such a thing as speaking about language.

J: But what we are doing now is evidence that there is such speaking.

I: All too much, I am afraid.

J: Then I do not understand why you hesitate.

I: Speaking *about* language turns language almost inevitably into an object.

J: And then its reality vanishes.

I: We then have taken up a position above language, instead
of hearing from it.

J: Then there would only be a speaking *from* language . . .

I: . . . in this manner, that it would be called *from out of*
language's reality, and be led *to* its reality.

J: How can we do that?

I: A speaking *from* language could only be a dialogue.

J: There is no doubt that we are moving in a dialogue.

I: But is it a dialogue *from out of* the nature of language?

J: It seems to me that now we are moving in a circle. A dialogue from language must be called for from out of language's reality. How can it do so, without first entering into
a hearing that at once reaches that reality?

I: I once called this strange relation the hermeneutic circle.

J: The circle exists everywhere in hermeneutics, that is to say,
according to your explanation of today, it exists where
the relation of message and message-bearer prevails.

I: The message-bearer must come from the message. But he
must also have gone toward it.

J: Did you not say earlier that this circle is inevitable, and
that, instead of trying to avoid it as an alleged logical con-
tradiction, we must follow it?

I: Yes. But this necessary acceptance of the hermeneutic circle
does not mean that the notion of the accepted circle gives
us an originary experience of the hermeneutic relation.

J: In short, you would abandon your earlier view.

I: Quite—and in this respect, that talk of a circle always remains superficial.

J: How would you present the hermeneutic circle today?

I: I would avoid a presentation as resolutely as I would avoid
speaking *about* language.

J: Then everything would hinge on reaching a corresponding saying of language.

I: Only a dialogue could be such a saying correspondence.

J: But, patently, a dialogue altogether *sui generis.*

I: A dialogue that would remain originarily appropriated to Saying.

J: But then, not every talk between people could be called a dialogue any longer . . .

I: . . . if we from now on hear this word as though it named for us a focusing on the reality of language.

J: In this sense, then, even Plato's *Dialogues* would not be dialogues?

I: I would like to leave that question open, and only point out that the kind of dialogue is determined by *that which* speaks to those who seemingly are the only speakers—men.

J: Wherever the nature of language were to speak (say) to man as Saying, *it,* Saying, would bring about the real dialogue . . .

I: . . . which does not say "about" language but *of* language, as needfully used of its very nature.

J: And it would also remain of minor importance whether the dialogue is before us in writing, or whether it was spoken at some time and has now faded.

I: Certainly—because the one thing that matters is whether this dialogue, be it written or spoken or neither, remains constantly coming.

J: The course of such a dialogue would have to have a character all its own, with more silence than talk.

I: Above all, silence about silence . . .

J: Because to talk and write about silence is what produces the most obnoxious chatter . . .

I: Who could simply be silent of silence?

J: That would be authentic saying . . .

I: . . . and would remain the constant prologue to the authentic dialogue *of* language.

J: Are we not attempting the impossible?

I: Indeed—so long as man has not yet been given the pure gift of the messenger's course that the message needs which grants to man the unconcealment of the two-fold.

J: To call forth this messenger's course, and still more to go it, seems to me incomparably more difficult than to discuss the nature of *Iki.*

I: Surely. For something would have to come about by which that vast distance in which the nature of Saying assumes its radiance, opened itself to the messenger's course and shone upon it.

J: A stilling would have to come about that quiets the breath of the vastness into the structure of Saying which calls out to the messenger.

I: The veiled relation of message and messenger's course *plays* everywhere.

J: In our ancient Japanese poetry, an unknown poet sings of the intermingling scent of cherry blossom and plum blossom on the same branch.

I: This is how I think of the being-toward-each-other of vastness and stillness in the same Appropriation of the message of unconcealment of the two-fold.

J: But who today could hear in it an echo of the nature of language which our word *Koto ba* names, flower petals that flourish out of the lightening message of the graciousness that brings forth?

I: Who would find in all this a serviceable clarification of the nature of language?

J: That nature will never be found as long as we demand information in the form of theorems and cue words.

I: Yet many a man could be drawn into the prologue to a messenger's course once he keeps himself ready for a dialogue of language.

J: It seems to me as though even we, now, instead of speaking about language, had tried to take some steps along a course which entrusts itself to the nature of Saying.

I: Which *promises,* dedicates itself to the nature of Saying. Let us be glad if it not only seems so but *is* so.

J: If it is so, what then?

I: Then the farewell of all "It is" comes to pass.

J: But you do not think of the farewell as a loss and denial, do you?

I: In no way.

J: But?

I: As the coming of what has been.

J: But what is past, goes, has gone—how can it come?

I: The passing of the past is something else than what has been.

J: How are we to think that?

I: As the gathering of what endures . . .

J: . . . which, as you said recently, endures as what grants endurance . . .

I: . . . and stays the Same as the message . . .

J: . . . which needs us as messengers.

THE NATURE OF LANGUAGE

THE NATURE OF LANGUAGE

I

The three lectures that follow bear the title "The Nature of Language." They are intended to bring us face to face with a possibility of undergoing an experience with language. To undergo an experience with something—be it a thing, a person, or a god—means that this something befalls us, strikes us, comes over us, overwhelms and transforms us. When we talk of "undergoing" an experience, we mean specifically that the experience is not of our own making; to undergo here means that we endure it, suffer it, receive it as it strikes us and submit to it. It is this something itself that comes about, comes to pass, happens.

To undergo an experience with language, then, means to let ourselves be properly concerned by the claim of language by entering into and submitting to it. If it is true that man finds the proper abode of his existence in language—whether he is aware of it or not—then an experience we undergo with language will touch the innnermost nexus of our existence. We who speak language may thereupon become transformed by such experiences, from one day to the next or in the course of time. But now it could be that an experience we

57

undergo with language is too much for us moderns, even if it strikes us only to the extent that for once it draws our attention to our *relation to language,* so that from then on we may keep this relation in mind.

Suppose, specifically, we were asked head-on: In what relation do you live to the language you speak? We should not be embarrassed for an answer. Indeed, we would at once discover a guideline and point of reference with which to lead the question into channels where it can safely be left.

We speak our language. How else can we be close to language except by speaking? Even so, our relation to language is vague, obscure, almost speechless. As we ponder this curious situation, it can scarcely be avoided that every observation on the subject will at first sound strange and incomprehensible. It therefore might be helpful to us to rid ourselves of the habit of always hearing only what we already understand. This my proposal is addressed not only to all those who listen; it is addressed still more to him who tries to speak of language, all the more when he does so with the sole intent to show possibilities that will allow us to become mindful of language and our relation to it.

But this, to undergo an experience with language, is something else again than to gather information about language. Such information—linguists and philologists of the most diverse languages, psychologists and analytic philosophers supply it to us, and constantly increase the supply, *ad infinitum.* Of late, the scientific and philosophical investigation of languages is aiming ever more resolutely at the production of what is called "metalanguage." Analytical philosophy, which is set on producing this super-language, is thus quite consistent when it considers itself metalinguistics. That sounds like metaphysics —not only sounds like it, it *is* metaphysics. Metalinguistics is the metaphysics of the thoroughgoing technicalization of all languages into the sole operative instrument of interplanetary information. Metalanguage and sputnik, metalinguistics and rocketry are the Same.

However, we must not give grounds for the impression that

we are here passing negative judgment on the scientific and philosophical investigation of language and of languages. Such investigation has its own particular justification and retains its own importance. But scientific and philosophical information about language is one thing; an experience we undergo with language is another. Whether the attempt to bring us face to face with the possibility of such an experience will succeed, and if it does, how far that possible success will go for each one of us—that is not up to any of us.

What is left for us to do is to point out ways that bring us face to face with a possibility of undergoing an experience with language. Such ways have long existed. But they are seldom used in such a manner that the possible experience with language is itself given voice and put into language. In experiences which we undergo *with* language, language itself brings itself to language. One would think that this happens anyway, any time anyone speaks. Yet at whatever time and in whatever way we speak a language, language itself never has the floor. Any number of things are given voice in speaking, above all what we are speaking about: a set of facts, an occurrence, a question, a matter of concern. Only because in everyday speaking language does *not* bring itself to language but holds back, are we able simply to go ahead and speak a language, and so to deal with something and negotiate something by speaking.

But when does language speak itself as language? Curiously enough, when we cannot find the right word for something that concerns us, carries us away, oppresses or encourages us. Then we leave unspoken what we have in mind and, without rightly giving it thought, undergo moments in which language itself has distantly and fleetingly touched us with its essential being.

But when the issue is to put into language something which has never yet been spoken, then everything depends on whether language gives or withholds the appropriate word. Such is the case of the poet. Indeed, a poet might even come to the point where he is compelled—in his own way, that is, poetically— to put into language the experience he undergoes with language.

Among Stefan George's late, simple, almost songlike poems there is one entitled "The Word." It was first published in 1919. Later it was included in the collection *Das Neue Reich*. The poem is made up of seven stanzas. The first three are clearly marked off from the next three, and these two triads as a whole are again marked off from the seventh, final stanza. The manner in which we shall here converse with this poem, briefly but throughout all three lectures, does not claim to be scientific. The poem runs:

> The Word
> Wonder or dream from distant land
> I carried to my country's strand
>
> And waited till the twilit norn
> Had found the name within her bourn—
>
> Then I could grasp it close and strong
> It blooms and shines now the front along . . .
>
> Once I returned from happy sail,
> I had a prize so rich and frail,
>
> She sought for long and tidings told:
> "No like of this these depths enfold."
>
> And straight it vanished from my hand,
> The treasure never graced my land . . .
>
> So I renounced and sadly see:
> Where word breaks off no thing may be.

After what we had noted earlier, we are tempted to concentrate on the poem's last line: "Where word breaks off no thing may be." For this line makes the word of language, makes language itself bring itself to language, and says something about the relation between word and thing. The content of the final line can be transformed into a statement, thus: "No thing is where the word breaks off." Where something breaks off, a breach, a diminution has occurred. To diminish means to take away, to cause a lack. "Breaks off" means "is lacking." No thing is where the word is lacking, that word which names the given thing. What does "to name" signify? We might answer: to name means to furnish something with a name. And what is a name? A designation that provides something with a vocal and written sign, a cipher. And what is a sign? Is it a signal? Or a token? A marker? Or a hint? Or all of these and something else besides? We have become very slovenly and mechanical in our understanding and use of signs.

Is the name, is the word a sign? Everything depends on how we think of what the words "sign" and "name" say. Even in these slight pointers we now begin to sense the drift that we are getting into when the word is put into language as word, language as language. That the poem, too, has *name* in mind when it says *word,* is said in the second stanza:

> And waited till the twilit norn
> Had found the name within her bourn—

Meanwhile, both the finder of the name, the norn of our poem, and the place where the name is found, her bourn, make us hesitant to understand "name" in the sense of a mere designation. It could be that the name and the naming word are here intended rather in the sense we know from such expressions as "in the name of the King" or "in the name of God." Gottfried Benn begins one of his poems: "In the name of him who bestows the hours." Here "in the name" says "at the call, by the command." The terms "name" and "word" in George's poem are thought differently and more deeply than as mere signs. But what am I saying? Is there thinking, too, going on in a poem? Quite so—in a poem of such rank thinking is going on, and indeed thinking without science, without philosophy. If that is true, then we may and in fact must, with all the self-restraint and circumspection that are called for, give more reflective thought to that closing line we first picked out from the poem "The Word."

> Where word breaks off no thing may be.

We ventured the paraphrase: No thing is where the word

is lacking. "Thing" is here understood in the traditional broad sense, as meaning anything that in any way *is*. In this sense even a god is a thing. Only where the word for the thing has been found is the thing a thing. Only thus *is* it. Accordingly we must stress as follows: no thing *is* where the word, that is, the name is lacking. The word alone gives being to the thing. Yet how can a mere word accomplish this—to bring a thing into being? The true situation is obviously the reverse. Take the sputnik. This thing, if such it is, *is* obviously independent of that name which was later tacked on to it. But perhaps matters are different with such things as rockets, atom bombs, reactors and the like, different from what the poet names in the first stanza of the first triad:

> Wonder or dream from distant land
> I carried to my country's strand

Still, countless people look upon this "thing" sputnik, too, as a wonder, this "thing" that races around in a worldless "world"—space; to many people it was and still is a dream—wonder and dream of this modern technology which would be the last to admit the thought that what gives things their being is the word. Actions not words count in the calculus of planetary calculation. What use are poets? And yet . . .

Let us for once refrain from hurried thinking. Is not even this "thing" what it is and the way it is in the name of its name? Certainly. If that hurry, in the sense of the technical maximization of all velocities, in whose time-space modern technology and apparatus can alone be what they are—if that hurry had not bespoken man and ordered him at its call, if that call to such hurry had not challenged him and put him at bay, if the word framing that order and challenge had not spoken: then there would be no sputnik. No thing is where the word is lacking. Thus the puzzle remains: the word of language and its relation to the thing, to every thing that is —that it is and the way it is.

This is why we consider it advisable to prepare for a possibility of undergoing an experience with language. This is why we listen now more attentively where such an experience is put into lofty and noble language. We listen to the poem that we read. Did we hear it? Barely. We have merely picked up the last line—and done so almost crudely—and have even ventured to rewrite it into an unpoetical statement: No thing is where the word is lacking. We could go further and propose this statement: something *is* only where the appropriate and therefore competent word names a thing as being, and so establishes the given being as a being. Does this mean, also, that there is being only where the appropriate word is speaking? Where does the word derive its appropriateness? The poet says nothing about it. But the content of the closing line does after all include the statement: The being of anything that is resides in the word. Therefore this statement holds true: Language is the house of Being. By this procedure, we would seem to have adduced from poetry the most handsome confirmation for a principle of thinking which we had stated at some time in the past—and in truth would have thrown everything into utter confusion. We would have reduced poetry to the servant's role as documentary proof for our thinking, and taken thinking too lightly; in fact we would already have forgotten the whole point: to undergo an experience with language.

Therefore, we now restore to integrity, in its original place in the poem's last stanza, the lines which we had first picked out and rewritten.

> So I renounced and sadly see:
> Where word breaks off no thing may be.

The poet, normally very sparing with his punctuation, has put a colon after "see." One would expect, then, something to follow which speaks in what the grammarians call direct discourse.

> So I renounced and sadly see:
> Where word breaks off no thing is.

But Stefan George does not say "is," he says "may be." In keeping with his practice elsewhere, he could omit the colon, an omission that would almost be more appropriate for the indirect discourse—if that is what it is—in the last line. Still, many precedents can be cited, presumably, for George's usage, for example a passage from Goethe's "Introduction to the Outline of a Theory of Color." There we find:

> In order that we may not appear overly timid by trying to avoid an explanation, we would revise what we said first, as follows: that color be an elementary natural phenomenon for the sense of sight. . . .

Goethe regards the words after the colon as the explanation of what color is, and says: "Color be . . . " But what is the situation in the last stanza of George's poem? Here we have to do not with a theoretical explanation of a natural phenomenon, but with a renunciation.

> So I renounced and sadly see:
> Where word breaks off no thing may be.

Do the words after the colon say what the substance of the renunciation is? Does the poet renounce the fact that no thing may be where the word breaks off? Exactly the opposite. The renunciation he has learned implies precisely that the poet admits that no thing may be where the word breaks off.

Why all these artful explications? The matter, after all, is clear. No, nothing is clear; but everything is significant. In what way? In this way, that what matters is for us to hear how, in the poem's last stanza, the whole of that experience is concentrated which the poet has undergone with the word —and that means with language as well; and that we must be careful not to force the vibration of the poetic saying into the rigid groove of a univocal statement, and so destroy it.

The last line, "Where word breaks off no thing may be," could then still have another meaning than that of a statement and affirmation put in indirect discourse, which says that no thing is where the word is lacking.

What follows the colon does not name what the poet renounces; rather, it names the realm into which the renunciation must enter; it names the call to enter into that relation between thing and word which has now been experienced. What the poet learned to renounce is his formerly cherished view regarding the relation of thing and word. His renunciation concerns the poetic relation to the word that he had cultivated until then. If so, the "may be" in the line, "Where word breaks off no thing may be," would grammatically speaking not be the subjunctive of "is," but a kind of imperative, a command which the poet follows, to keep it from then on. If so, the "may be" in the line, "Where word breaks off no thing may be," would mean: do not henceforth admit any thing as being where the word breaks off. In the "may be" understood as a command, the poet avows to himself the self-denial he has learned, in which he abandons the view that something may be even if and even while the word for it is still lacking. What does renunciation mean? It is equivalent to "abdication." Here the root word is the Latin *dicere,* to say, the Greek *deiknumi,* to show, point out, indicate. In his renunciation, the poet abdicates his former relation to the word. Nothing more? No. There is in the abdication itself already an avowal, a command to which he denies himself no longer.

Now it would be just as forced to claim that the imperative interpretation of "may be" is the only possible one. Presumably one meaning and the other of "may be" vibrate and mingle in the poetic saying: a command as appeal, and submission to it.

The poet has learned renunciation. He has undergone an experience. With what? With the thing and its relation to the word. But the title of the poem is simply "The Word." The decisive experience is that which the poet has undergone with the word—and with the word inasmuch as it alone can bestow a relation to a thing. Stated more explicitly, the poet has experienced that only the word makes a thing appear as the thing it is, and thus lets it be present. The word avows itself to the poet as that which holds and sustains a thing in its being. The poet experiences an authority, a dignity of the word than which nothing vaster and loftier can be thought. But the word is also that possession with which the poet is trusted and entrusted as poet in an extraordinary way. The poet experiences his poetic calling as a call to the word as the source, the bourn of Being. The renunciation which the poet learns is of that special kind of fulfilled self-denial to which alone is promised what has long been concealed and is essentially vouchsafed already.

The poet, then, ought to rejoice at such an experience, which brings to him the most joyful gift a poet can receive. Instead, the poem says: "So I renounced and sadly see." The poet, then, is merely depressed by his renunciation because it means a loss. Yet, as we have seen, the renunciation is not a loss. Nor does "sadly" refer to the substance of the renunciation, but rather to the fact that he has learned it. That sadness, however, is neither mere dejection nor despondency. True sadness is in harmony with what is most joyful—but in this way, that the greatest joy withdraws, halts in its withdrawal, and holds itself in reserve. By learning that renunciation, the poet undergoes his experience with the word's lofty sway. He receives primal knowledge of what task is assigned to the poetic saying, what sublime and lasting matters are promised to it and yet withheld from it. The poet could never go through the experience he undergoes with the word if the experience were not attuned to sadness, to the mood of releasement into the nearness of what is withdrawn but at the same time held in reserve for an originary advent.

These few pointers may suffice to make it clearer what experience the poet has undergone with language. Experience means *eundo assequi,* to obtain something along the way, to attain something by going on a way. What is it that the poet reaches? Not mere knowledge. He obtains entrance into the relation of word to thing. This relation is not, however, a connection between the thing that is on one side and the word that is on the other. The word itself is the relation which in each instance retains the thing within itself in such a manner that it "is" a thing.

And yet, in making these statements, however broad their implications, we have done no more than sum up the experience the poet has undergone with the word, instead of entering into the experience itself. How did the experience happen? We are guided toward the answer by that one little word which we have neglected so far in our discussion of the poem's final stanza:

> So I renounced and sadly see:
> Where word breaks off no thing may be.

"*So* I renounced . . ." How? In the way the first six stanzas say it. What we have just noted concerning the last stanza may shed some light on the first six. They must speak for themselves, of course, from within the totality of the poem.

In these six stanzas there speaks the experience that the poet undergoes with language. Something comes to pass for him, strikes him, and transforms his relation to the word. It is thus necessary first to mention the relation to language in which the poet stood *before* the experience. It speaks in the first three stanzas. The last line of the third stanza trails off in an ellipsis, and so marks off the first triad from the second. The fourth stanza then opens the second triad—rather abruptly, with the word "Once," taken here in its primary meaning: one time. The second triad tells what the poet experiences once and for all. To experience is to go along a way. The way leads through a landscape. The poet's land belongs within that landscape, as does the dwelling of the twilit norn, ancient goddess of fate. She dwells on the strand, the edge of the poetic land which is itself a boundary, a march. The twilit norn watches over her bourn, the well in whose depths she searches for the names she would bring forth from it. Word, language, belongs within the domain of this mysterious landscape in which poetic saying borders on the fateful source of speech. At first, and for long, it seems as though the poet needed only to bring the wonders that enthrall and the dreams that enrapture him to the well-spring of language, and there in unclouded confidence let the words come forth to him that fit all the wonderful and dream-like things whose images have come to him. In a former time,

the poet, emboldened as his poems turned out well, cherished
the view that the poetic things, the wonders and dreams, had,
even on their own, their well-attested standing within Being,
and that no more was necessary than that his art now also find
the word for them to describe and present them. At first, and
for long, it seemed as though a word were like a grasp that
fastens upon the things already in being and held to be in
being, compresses and expresses them, and thus makes them
beautiful.

> Wonder or dream from distant land
> I carried to my country's strand
>
> And waited till the twilit norn
> Had found the name within her bourn—
>
> Then I could grasp it close and strong
> It blooms and shines now the front along . . .

Wonders and dreams on the one hand, and on the other
hand the names by which they are grasped, and the two fused—
thus poetry came about. Did this poetry do justice to what is
in the poet's nature—that he must found what is lasting, in
order that it may endure and be?

But in the end the moment comes for Stefan George when
the conventional self-assured poetic production suddenly breaks
down and makes him think of Hölderlin's words:

> But what endures is founded by poets.

For at one time, once, the poet—still filled with hope after a
happy sail—reaches the place of the ancient goddess of fate and
demands the name of the rich and frail prize that lies there
plain in his hand. It is neither "wonder from afar" nor
"dream." The goddess searches long, but in vain. She gives
him the tidings:

> "No like of this these depths enfold."

There is nothing in these depths that is like the prize so rich
and frail which is plainly there in his hand. Such a word, which
would let the prize lying there plainly be what it is—such a

word would have to well up out of the secure depths reposing
in the stillness of deep slumber. Only a word from such a
source could keep the prize secure in the richness and frailty of
its simple being.

"No like of this these depths enfold."

And straight it vanished from my hand,
The treasure never graced my land . . .

The frail rich prize, already plainly in hand, does not reach
being as a thing, it does not come to be a treasure, that is, a
poetically secured possession of the land. The poet remains
silent about the prize which could not become a treasure of
his land, but which yet granted to him an experience with
language, the opportunity to learn the renunciation in whose
self-denial the relation of word to thing promises itself to him.
The "prize so rich and frail" is contrasted with "wonder or
dream from distant land." If the poem is a poetic expression
of Stefan George's own poetic way, we may surmise that the
prize he had in mind was that sensitive abundance of simplicity which comes to the poet in his late years as what needs
and assents to be said. The poem itself, which has turned out
well, a lyric song of language, proves that he did learn the
renunciation.

But as for us, it must remain open whether we are capable
of entering properly into this poetic experience. There is the
danger that we will overstrain a poem such as this by thinking
too much into it, and thereby debar ourselves from being
moved by its poetry. Much greater of course—but who today
would admit it?—is the danger that we will think too little,
and reject the thought that the true experience wih language
can only be a thinking experience, all the more so because the
lofty poetry of all great poetic work always vibrates within a
realm of thinking. But if what matters first of all is a thinking
experience with language, then why this stress on a poetic
experience? Because thinking in turn goes its ways in the
neighborhood of poetry. It is well, therefore, to give thought

to the neighbor, to him who dwells in the same neighborhood. Poetry and thought, each needs the other in its neighborhood, each in its fashion, when it comes to ultimates. In what region the neighborhood itself has its domain, each of them, thought and poetry, will define differently, but always so that they will find themselves within the same domain. But because we are caught in the prejudice nurtured through centuries that thinking is a matter of ratiocination, that is, of calculation in the widest sense, the mere talk of a neighborhood of thinking to poetry is suspect.

Thinking is not a means to gain knowledge. Thinking cuts furrows into the soil of Being. About 1875, Nietzsche once wrote (Grossoktav WW XI, 20): "Our thinking should have a vigorous fragrance, like a wheatfield on a summer's night." How many of us today still have the senses for that fragrance?

By now, the two opening sentences of our lecture can be restated more clearly. This series of lectures bears the title "The Nature of Language." It is intended to bring us face to face with a possibility of undergoing a thinking experience with language. Be it noted that we said a possibility. We are still only in the preliminaries, in an attempt, even though the title does not say so. That title, "The Nature of Language," sounds rather presumptuous, as though we were about to promulgate reliable information concerning the nature of language. Besides, the title sounds altogether too trite, like "The Nature of Art," "The Nature of Freedom," "The Nature of Technology," "The Nature of Truth," "The Nature of Religion," etc. etc. We are all getting somewhat surfeited with all this big production of natures, for reasons which we do not quite understand ourselves. But what if we were to get rid of the presumptuousness and triteness of the title by a simple device? Let us give the title a question mark, such that the whole of it is covered by that mark and hence has a different sound. It then runs: The Nature?—of Language? Not only language is in question now, but so is the meaning of nature— and what is more, the question now is whether and in what way nature (essential being) and language belong together.

The Nature?—of Language? With the addition of the questions marks, all of the title's presumptuousness and triteness vanish. At the same time, one question calls forth the others. The following two questions arise at once:

How are we to put questions to language when our relation to it is muddled, in any case undefined? How can we inquire about its nature, when it may immediately become a matter of dispute what nature means?

No matter how many ways we may devise to get our inquiry into language and the investigation of its nature started, all our efforts will be in vain as long as we close our minds in one very important respect which by no means concerns only the questions here touched upon.

If we put questions to language, questions about its nature, its being, then clearly language itself must already have been granted to us. Similarly, if we want to inquire into the being of language, then that which is called nature or being must also be already granted to us. Inquiry and investigation here and everywhere require the prior grant of whatever it is they approach and pursue with their queries. Every posing of every question takes place within the very grant of what is put in question.

What do we discover when we give sufficient thought to the matter? This, that the authentic attitude of thinking is not a putting of questions—rather, it is a listening to the grant, the promise of what is to be put in question. But in the history of our thinking, asking questions has since the early days been regarded as the characteristic procedure of thinking, and not without good cause. Thinking is more thoughtful in proportion as it takes a more radical stance, as it goes to the *radix*, the root of all that is. The quest of thinking always remains the search for the first and ultimate grounds. Why? Because this, that something is and what it is, the persistent presence of being, has from of old been determined to be the ground and foundation. As all nature has the character of a ground, a search for it is the founding and grounding of the ground or foundation. A thinking that thinks in the direction of nature defined in this way is fundamentally a questioning. At the close of a lecture called "The Question of Technology," given some time ago, I said: "Questioning is the piety of thinking." "Piety" is meant here in the ancient sense: obedient, or submissive, and in this case submitting to what thinking has to think about. One of the exciting experiences of thinking is that at times it does not fully comprehend the new insights it has just gained, and does not properly see them through. Such, too, is the case with the sentence just cited that questioning is the piety of thinking. The lecture ending with that sentence was already in the ambiance of the realization that the true stance of thinking cannot be to put questions, but must be to listen to that which our questioning vouchsafes—and all questioning begins to be a questioning only in virtue of pursuing its quest for essential being. Accordingly, the title of these lectures, even if we provide it with a question mark, does not thereby alone become the title for an experience of thinking. But there it is, waiting to be completed in terms of what we have just remarked concerning the true attitude of thinking. No matter how we' put our questions to language about its nature, first of all it is needful that language vouchsafe itself to us. If it does, the nature of language becomes the grant of its essential being, that is, the being of language becomes the language of being.

Our title, "The Nature of Language," has now lost even its role as title. What it says is the echo of a thinking experience, the possibility of which we are trying to bring before us: the being of language—the language of being.

In the event that this statement—if that is what it is— represents not merely a contrived and hence vacuous inversion, the possibility may emerge that we shall at the proper time substitute another word for "language" as well as for "nature."

The whole that now addresses us—the being of language: the language of being—is not a title, let alone an answer to a question. It becomes a guide word, meant to guide us on our way. On that way of thinking, the poetic experience with the word which we heard at the beginning is to be our companion.

We have already had converse with it, we recall, with this result: the closing line, "Where word breaks off no thing may be," points to the relation of word and thing in this manner, that the word itself is the relation, by holding everything forth into being, and there upholding it. If the word did not have this bearing, the whole of things, the "world," would sink into obscurity, including the "I" of the poem, him who brings to his country's strand, to the source of names, all the wonders and dreams he encounters.

In order that we may hear the voice of Stefan George's poetic experience with the word once more in another key, I shall in closing read Gottfried Benn's two-stanza poem.* The tone of this poem is tauter and at the same time more vehement, because it is abandoned and at the same time resolved in the extreme. The poem's title is a characteristic and presumably intentional variation:

A Word

A word, a phrase—: from cyphers rise
Life recognized, a sudden sense,
The sun stands still, mute are the skies,
And all compacts it, stark and dense.

A word—a gleam, a flight, a spark,
A thrust of flames, a stellar trace—
And then again—immense—the dark
Round world and I in empty space.

II

These three lectures are intended to bring us face to face with a possibility of undergoing an experience with language. To experience something means to attain it along the way, by going on a way. To undergo an experience with something means that this something, which we reach along the way in order to attain it, itself pertains to us, meets and makes its

* The translation, by Richard Exner, is taken from Gottfried Benn, *Primal Vision*, edited by E. B. Ashton, p. 251. Reprinted by permission of New Directions Publishing Corporation. All rights reserved. (Tr.)

appeal to us, in that it transforms us into itself.

Because our goal is to experience, to be underway, let us give thought to the way today, in this lecture leading from the first over to the third lecture. But because most of you here are primarily engaged in scientific thinking, a prefatory remark will be in order. The sciences know the way to knowledge by the term "method." Method, especially in today's modern scientific thought, is not a mere instrument serving the sciences; rather, it has pressed the sciences into its own service. Nietzsche was the first to recognize this situation, with all its vast implications, and to give it expression in the notes that follow. These notes are found in his literary remains, as numbers 466 and 469 of *The Will to Power*. The first note runs: "It is not the victory of *science* that distinguishes our nineteenth century, but the victory of scientific *method* over science."

The other note begins with this sentence: "The most valuable insights are gained last of all; but the most valuable insights are the *methods*."

Nietzsche himself, too, gained this insight into the relation of method to science last of all—to wit, in the last year of his lucid life, 1888, in Turin.

In the sciences, not only is the theme drafted, called up by the method, it is also set up within the method and remains within the framework of the method, subordinated to it. The furious pace at which the sciences are swept along today—they themselves don't know whither—comes from the speed-up drive of method with all its potentialities, a speed-up that is more and more left to the mercy of technology. Method holds all the coercive power of knowledge. The theme is a part of the method.

But in thinking, the situation is different from that of scientific representation. In thinking there is neither method nor theme, but rather the region, so called because it gives its realm and free reign* to what thinking is given to think. Thinking abides in that country, walking the ways of that country. Here

---

* "*die Gegend . . . gegnet*"; for Heidegger's own remarks on his use of the word, see his *Discourse on Thinking* (tr. J. M. Anderson & E. H. Freund; New York: Harper & Row, 1966), pp. 65-66. (Tr.)

the way is part of the country and belongs to it. From the point of view of the sciences, it is not just difficult but impossible to see this situation. If in what follows we reflect, then, upon the way of thoughtful experience with language, we are not undertaking a methodological consideration. We are even now walking in that region, the realm that concerns us.

We speak and speak about language. What we speak of, language, is always ahead of us. Our speaking merely follows language constantly. Thus we are continually lagging behind what we first ought to have overtaken and taken up in order to speak about it. Accordingly, when we speak of language we remain entangled in a speaking that is persistently inadequate. This tangle debars us from the matters that are to make themselves known to our thinking. But this tangle, which our thinking must never take too lightly, drops away as soon as we take notice of the peculiar properties of the way of thought, that is, as soon as we look about us in the country where thinking abides. This country is everywhere open to the neighborhood of poetry.

As we give our mind to the way of thinking, we must give thought to this neighborhood. Taken at its surface value and recounted, our first lecture deals with three matters:

First, it points to a poetic experience with language. The pointer is limited to a few remarks about Stefan George's poem "The Word."

Next, the lecture characterizes the experience, which to prepare is our task here, as a thinking experience. Where thinking finds its way to its true destination, it comes to a focus in listening to the promise that tells us what there is for thinking to think upon.

Every question posed to the matter of thinking, every inquiry for its nature, is already borne up by the grant of what is to come into question. Therefore the proper bearing of the thinking which is needed now is to listen to the grant, not to ask questions. But since such listening is a listening for the countering word, our listening to the grant for what we are to think always develops into our asking for the answer. Our characterization of thinking as a listening sounds strange, nor is it sufficiently clear for our present needs. However, this is what constitutes the peculiarity of listening: it receives its definiteness and clarity from what indications the grant gives to it. But one thing is clear even now: the listening we have now in mind tends toward the grant, as Saying to which the nature of language is akin. If we succeed in gaining insight into the possibility of a thinking experience with language, it might clarify the sense in which thinking is a listening to the grant.*

Finally, the first lecture covers a third point, the transformation of the title of our lecture series. The transformation begins by removing the title's presumptuousness and triteness, by adding a question mark which puts both language and essential being into question, and turns the title into a query: *The Nature?—of Language?*

Now the point of our attempt is to prepare a thinking experience with language. But since to think is before all else to listen, to let ourselves be told something and not to ask questions, we must strike the question mark out again when a thinking experience is at stake, and yet we can no longer simply return to the original form of the title. If we are to think through the nature of language, language must first promise itself to us, or must already have done so. Language must, in its own way, avow to us itself—its nature. Language persists as this avowal. We hear it constantly, of course, but do not give it thought. If we did not hear it everywhere, we could not use one single word of language. Language is active as this promise. The essential nature of language makes itself known to us as what is spoken, the language of its nature. But we cannot quite hear this primal knowledge, let alone "read" it. It runs: The being of language—the language of being.**

What we have just said is an imposition. If it were merely

---

*"... in welchem Sinne das Denken ein Hören der Zusage ist." *Zusage* as here used by Heidegger exceeds the meaning of the translation "grant." *Zusage* is a *Sage*, a Saying. To put it brutally: Being *says*, and language follows Saying in speech. (Tr.)

**"Das Wesen der Sprache: Die Sprache des Wesens." The context here seems to demand the translation "being" for *Wesen*, otherwise translated variously: nature, essential nature, or essence. (Tr.)

an assertion, we could set out to prove its truth or falseness. That would be easier by far than to endure the imposition or make our peace with it.

The being of language—the language of being. The demand that we experience this sentence thoughtfully would seem to stem from the lecture imposing it on us. But the imposition comes from another source. The transformation of the title is of such a kind that it makes the title disappear. What follows then is not a dissertation on language under a different heading. What follows is the attempt to take our first step into the country which holds possibilities of a thinking experience with language in readiness for us. In that country, thinking encounters its neighborhood with poetry. We heard of a poetic experience with the word. It is concentrated in the language of the poem's last stanza:

> So I renounced and sadly see:
> Where word breaks off no thing may be.

Through a brief commentary on the two preceding triads, we tried to gain an insight into the poetic way of this experience. Just a look from afar at the poet's way—surely we are not conceited enough to imagine that we have gone this way ourselves. For George's poetic saying, in this poem and in the others that belong with it, is a going that is like a going away, after the poet had formerly spoken like a lawgiver and a herald. Thus this poem "The Word" rightly has its place in the last part of the last volume of poetry George published, *Das Neue Reich,* published in 1928. This last part is entitled "The Song." The song is sung, not after it has come to be, but rather: in the singing the song begins to be a song. The song's poet is the singer. Poetry is song. Hölderlin, following the example of the ancients, likes to call poetry "song."

In his recently discovered hymn "Celebration of Peace," Hölderlin sings, at the beginning of the eighth stanza:

> Much, from the morning onwards,
> Since we have been a discourse and have heard from
>   one another,
> Has human kind learnt; but soon we shall be song.*

Those who "have heard from one another"—the ones and the others—are men and gods. The song celebrates the advent of the gods—and in that advent everything falls silent. Song is not the opposite of a discourse, but rather the most intimate kinship with it; for song, too, is language. In the preceding seventh stanza, Hölderlin says:

> This is a law of fate, that each shall know all others,
> That when the silence returns there shall be a language too.

In 1910, Norbert von Hellingrath, who was killed in action before Verdun in 1916, first published Hölderlin's Pindar translations from the manuscripts. In 1914, there followed the first publication of Hölderlin's late hymns. These two books hit us students like an earthquake. Stefan George, who had first directed Hellingrath's attention to Hölderlin, now in turn received decisive inspiration from those first editions, as did Rilke. Since that time, George's poetry comes closer and closer to song. Nietzsche's words in the third part of *Thus Spoke Zarathustra*, at the end of "The Great Longing," are even then ringing in the poet's ear:

> O my soul, now I have given you all, and even the last I had,
> and I have emptied all my hands to you: *that I bade you sing,*
> behold, that was the last I had.

The final section of George's *Das Neue Reich*, below the section title *"The Song,"* begins with this motto:

> What I still ponder, and what I still frame,
> What I still love—their features are the same.

The poet has stepped outside of his former "circle," yet without renouncing the word; for he sings, and song remains discourse. The poet's renunciation does not touch the word, but rather

---

*Translation by Michael Hamburger, from *Friedrich Hölderlin: Poems and Fragments* (Ann Arbor, 1966), p. 439. (Tr.)

the relation of word to thing, more precisely: the mysterious-
ness of that relation, which reveals itself as mystery at just that
point where the poet wants to name a prize which he holds
plainly in his hand. The poet does not say what sort of prize
it is. We may recall that "prize" means a small and graceful
gift intended for one's guest; or perhaps a present in token of
special favor, which the recipient will henceforth carry on his
person. "Prize," then, has to do with favor and with guest. Let
us note also that that other poem, "Sea Song," together with
"The Word," belongs under the heading "The Song" of the
volume's last section. "Sea Song" begins:

> When on the verge with gentle fall
> Down dips the fire-reddened ball:
> Then on the dunes I pause to rest
> That I may see a cherished guest.

The last line names the guest, yet does not name him. Like the
guest, the prize remains nameless. And nameless remains also
that highest favor which comes to the poet. The last poem in
this last section has its say about the favor, sings it, but still
does not name it.

Prize, favor, guest, it says—but they are not named. Are they
then kept secret? No. We can keep secret only what we know.
The poet does not keep the names a secret. He does not know
them. He admits it himself in that one verse which rings like a
basso ostinato through all the songs:

> Wherein you hang—you do not know.

The experience of this poet with the word passes into darkness,
and even remains veiled itself. We must leave it so; but merely
by thinking about the poetic experience in this way, we leave
it in the neighborhood of thinking. However, we may not
suppose that a thinking experience with language, rather than
the poetic experience, will lead us to the light more quickly,
and perhaps could lift the veil. What thinking can do here
depends on whether and in what way it hears the granting
saying in which the being of language speaks as the language

of being. However, it is not merely an expedient that our attempt to prepare for a thinking experience with language seeks out the neighborhood of poetry; for the attempt rests upon the supposition that poetry and thinking belong within one neighborhood. Perhaps this supposition corresponds to the imposition which we hear only vaguely so far: the being of language—the language of being.

In order to uncover a possibility of undergoing a thinking experience with language, let us seek out the neighborhood in which poetry and thinking dwell. A strange beginning—we have so little experience with either. And yet we know them both. A great many things are known to us about poetry and thinking under the rubrics *Poetry* and *Philosophy*. Nor are we trying to find our way blindly into the neighborhood of poetry and thinking; a poem "The Word" is already echoing in our ears, and thus we have our eyes on a poetic experience with language. With all due reservations we may sum it up in the saying of the renunciation: "Where word breaks off no thing may be." As soon as we consider that what is named here is the relation between thing and word, and with it the relation of language to an entity as such, we have called poetry over into the neighborliness of thinking. Thinking, however, sees nothing strange in that. In fact, the relation between thing and word is among the earliest matters to which Western thinking gives voice and word, and does so in the form of the relation between being and saying. This relation assaults thinking in such an overpowering manner that it announces itself in a single word. The word is *logos*. It speaks simultaneously as the name for Being and for Saying.

More overpowering still for us is the fact that here no thinking experience with language is being made, in the sense that language itself, as such, comes to word explicitly and according to that relation. From this observation we conclude: Stefan George's poetic experience means something age-old, something that has struck thinking long ago and ever since has held it captive, though in a manner that has become both commonplace and indiscernible to us. Neither poetic experience with the word nor the thinking experience with Saying gives voice to language in its essential being.

Such is the situation, and this despite the fact that since the early days of Western thinking, and up into the late period of Stefan George's poetic work, thinking has thought deep thoughts about language, and poetry has made stirring things into language. But we can only conjecture why it is that, nonetheless, the being of language nowhere brings itself to word as the language of being. There is some evidence that the essential nature of language flatly refuses to express itself in words—in the language, that is, in which we make statements about language. If language everywhere withholds its nature in this sense, then such withholding is in the very nature of language. Thus language not only holds back when we speak it in the accustomed ways, but this its holding back is determined by the fact that language holds back its own origin and so denies its being to our usual notions. But then we may no longer say that the being of language is the language of being, unless the word "language" in the second phrase says something different, in fact something in which the withholding of the being of language—speaks. Accordingly, the being of language puts inself into language nonetheless, in its own most appropriate manner. We may avoid the issue no longer; rather, we must keep on conjecturing what the reason may be why the peculiar speech of language's being passes unnoticed all too easily. Presumably part of the reason is that the two kinds of utterance *par excellence,* poetry and thinking, have not been sought out in their proper habitat, their neighborhood. Yet we talk often enough about "poets and thinkers."* By now, this phrase has become a vacuous cliché. Perhaps the "and" in "poetry and thinking" will receive its full meaning and definition if we will let it enter our minds that this "and" might signify the neighborhood of poetry and thought.

We will, of course, immediately demand an explanation of

* The characterization of the Germans as "the people of poets and thinkers," familiar to every German schoolboy, is of uncertain origin, though it is found in German literature as early as 1808. (Tr.)

what "neighborhood" is supposed to mean here, and by what right we talk about such a thing. A neighbor, as the word itself tells us, is someone who dwells near to and with someone else. This someone else thereby becomes himself the neighbor of the one. Neighborhood, then, is a relation resulting from the fact that the one settles face to face with the other. Accordingly, the phrase of the neighborhood of poetry and thinking means that the two dwell face to face with each other, that the one has settled facing the other, has drawn into the other's nearness. This remark about what makes a neighborhood is by way of figurative talk. Or are we already saying something to the point? What, really, does "figurative talk" mean? We are quick to give the answer, never giving it a thought that we cannot claim to have a reliable formulation so long as it remains unclear what is talk and what is imagery, and in what way language speaks in images, if indeed language does speak so at all. Therefore we will here leave everything wide open. Let us stay with the most urgent issue, which is, to seek out the neighborhood of poetry and thinking—which now means the encounter of the two facing each other.

Fortunately we do not need either to search for this neighborhood or to seek it out. We are already abiding in it. We move within it. The poet's poem speaks to us. In our encounter with the poem, we have thought out a few things, though only in crude approximation.

Where word breaks off no thing may be

is what the poet's renunciation says; we added that here the relation between thing and word comes to light, and further that thing here means anything that in any way has being, any being as such. About the "word" we also said that it not only stands in a relation to the thing, but that the word is what first brings that given thing, as the being that is, into this "is"; that the word is what holds the thing there and relates it and so to speak provides its maintenance with which to be a thing. Accordingly, we said, the word not only stands in a relation to the thing, but this "may be" itself is what holds, relates, and keeps the thing as thing; that the "may be," as such keeper, is the relation itself.

These thoughts about the poem may to some seem super-fluous, importunate, and forced. But the point here is to find, in the neighborhood of the poetic experience with the word, a possibility for a *thinking* experience with language. That means now and first: we must learn to heed that neighborhood itself in which poetry and thinking have their dwelling. But, strangely—the neighborhood itself remains invisible. The same thing happens in our daily lives. We live in a neighborhood, and yet we would be baffled if we had to say in what that neighborhood consists. But this perplexity is merely a particular case, though perhaps an exceptionally good one, of the old encompassing perplexity in which all our thinking and saying finds itself always and everywhere. What is this perplexity we have in mind? This: we are not in a position—or if we are, then only rarely and just barely—to experience purely in its own terms a relation that obtains between two things, two beings. We immediately conceive the relation in terms of the things which in the given instance are related. We little understand how, in what way, by what means, and from where the relation comes about, and what it properly is *qua* relation. It remains correct, of course, to conceive of a neighborhood as a relation; and this notion applies also to the neighborhood of poetry and thinking. But the notion tells us nothing about whether poetry draws into the neighborhood of thinking, or thinking into that of poetry, or whether both are drawn into each other's neighborhood. Poetry moves in the element of saying, and so does thinking. When we reflect on poetry, we find ourselves at once in that same element in which thinking moves. We cannot here decide flatly whether poetry is really a kind of thinking, or thinking really a kind of poetry. It remains dark to us what determines their real relation, and from what source what we so casually call the "real" really comes. But—no matter how we call poetry and thought to mind, in every case one and the same element has drawn close to us—saying—whether we pay attention to it or not.

There is still more: poetry and thinking not only move within the element of saying, they also owe their saying to manifold experiences with language, experiences which we have hardly noticed, let alone collected. Where we did notice and collect them, we did so without adequate regard for just what concerns us more and more closely in our present reflections: the neighborhood of poetry and thinking. Presumably this neighborhood is not a mere result after all, brought about only by the fact that poetry and thinking draw together into a face-to-face encounter; for the two belong to each other even before they ever could set out to come face to face one to the other. Saying is the same element for both poetry and thinking; but for both it was and still remains "element" in a different way than water is the element for the fish, or air for the bird—in a way that compels us to stop talking about element, since Saying does more than merely "bear up" poetry and thinking, more than afford them the region they traverse.

All this is easily said, that is, put into words, to be sure, but difficult to experience especially for us moderns. What we try to reflect upon under the name of the neighborhood of poetry and thinking is vastly different from a mere inventory of notional relations. The neighborhood in question pervades everywhere our stay on this earth and our journey in it. But since modern thinking is ever more resolutely and exclusively turning into calculation, it concentrates all available energy and "interests" in calculating how man may soon establish himself in worldless cosmic space. This type of thinking is about to abandon the earth as earth. As calculation, it drifts more and more rapidly and obsessively toward the conquest of cosmic space. This type of thinking is itself already the explosion of a power that could blast everything to nothingness. All the rest that follows from such thinking, the technical processes in the functioning of the doomsday machinery, would merely be the final sinister dispatch of madness into senselessness. As early as 1917, Stefan George, in his great ode "The war" written during the First World War, said: "These are the fiery signs—not the tidings" (*Das Neue Reich*, p. 29) .

Our attempt to see the neighborhood itself of poetry and thinking has faced us with a peculiar difficulty. If we were thoughtless enough to let it pass, the distance that these lectures cover and our progress along that way would remain hazy. The difficulty is reflected in what has already brushed us in the first lecture, and meets us head-on in the present lecture.

When we listen to the poet and, in our own fashion, consider what his renunciation says, we are already staying in the neighborhood of poetry and thinking; and yet again we are not, at least not so that we experience the neighborhood as such. We are not yet on our way to it. We must first turn, turn back to where we are in reality already staying. The abiding turn, back to where we already are, is infinitely harder than are hasty excursions to places where we are not yet and never will be, except perhaps as the monstrous creatures of technology, assimilated to machines.

The step back into the sphere of human being demands other things than does the progress into the machine world.

To turn back to where we are (in reality) already staying: that is how we must walk along the way of thinking which now becomes necessary. If we pay attention to the peculiar property of this way, the at first troublesome semblance of an entanglement fades away. We speak of language, but constantly seem to be speaking merely *about* language, while in fact we are already letting language, *from within* language, speak to us, in language, of itself, saying its nature. This is why we must not prematurely break off the dialogue we have begun with the poetic experience we have heard, for fear that thinking would not allow poetry to find its own words any longer, but would force everything into the way of thinking.

We must dare to move back and forth within the neighborhood of the poem, and of its closing stanza into which the poem gathers. We try anew to hear what is being said poetically. We shall assume that demands may be made on thinking, and with that we begin.

So I renounced and sadly see:
Where word breaks off no thing may be.

Once again we revise the last line in such a way that it sounds almost like a statement, even a theorem: No thing is where the word is lacking. A thing is not until, and is only where, the word is not lacking but *is* there. But if the word is, then it must itself also be a thing, because "thing" here means whatever is in some way: "Wonder or dream from distant land." Or could it be that when the word speaks, *qua* word it is not a thing—in no way like what is? Is the word a nothing? But then how is it supposed to help the thing to be? Whatever bestows being, must it not "be" itself, all the more and before all else, be most in being, more so than all the things that are? We cannot see it any other way as long as we calculate, that is, compute the sufficient reason which rationalizes beings as the result of reason, reason's effects, and thereby satisfies our conceptualizations. Accordingly, if the word is to endow the thing with being, it too must be before any thing is—thus it must inescapably be itself a thing. We would then be faced with the situation that one thing, the word, conveys being to another thing. But, says the poet, "Where word breaks off no thing may be." Word and thing are different, even disparate. We suppose that we have understood the poet on first hearing; but no sooner have we so to speak touched the line thoughtfully than what it says fades away into darkness. The word, which itself is supposed not to be a thing, not anything that "is," escapes us. It seems as though what is happening here is just like what happens with the prize in the poem. Does the poet perhaps mean that the "prize so rich and frail" is the word itself? In that case Stefan George, sensing with a poet's intuition that the word itself could not be a thing, would have asked the norn to give the word for the prize, for the word itself. But the goddess of fate tells him, "No like of this these depths enfold."

The word for the word can never be found in that place where fate provides the language that names and so endows all beings, so that they may be, radiant and flourishing in their being. The word for the word is truly a prize, yet it can never be won for the poet's land. Can it be won for thinking? When thinking tries to pursue the poetic word, it turns out that the word, that saying has no being. Yet our current notions resist such an imputation. Everybody, after all, sees and hears words in writing and in sound. They are; they can be like things, palpable to the senses. To offer a crude example, we only need to open a dictionary. It is full of printed things. Indeed, all kinds of things. Plenty of terms, and not a single word, Because a dictionary can neither grasp nor keep the word by which the terms become words and speak as words. Where does the word, where does Saying belong?

Thus the poetic experience with the word gives us a meaningful hint. The word—no thing, nothing that is, no being; but we have an understanding of things when the word for them is available. Then the thing "is." Yet, what about this "is"? The thing is. The "is" itself—is it also a thing, a step above the other, set on top of it like a cap? The "is" cannot be found anywhere as a thing attached to a thing. As with the word, so it is with the "is." It belongs no more among the things that are than does the word.

Of a sudden, we are awakening from the slumber of hastily formed opinions, and are struck by the sight of something other.

What the poetic experience with language says of the word implies the relation beween the "is" which itself is not, and the word which is in the same case of not being a being.

Neither the "is" nor the word attain to thinghood, to Being, nor does the relation between "is" and the word, the word whose task it is to give an "is" in each given instance. But even so, neither the "is" nor the word and its Saying can be cast out into the void of mere nothingness. What, then, does the poetic experience with the word show as our thinking pursues it? It points to something thought-provoking and memorable with which thinking has been charged from the beginning, even though in a veiled mannner. It shows what is there and yet "is" not. The word, too, belongs to what is

there—perhaps not merely "too" but first of all, and even in
such a way such that the word, the nature of the word, conceals within itself that which gives being. If our thinking
does justice to the matter, then we may never say of the word
that it is, but rather that it gives—not in the sense that words
are given by an "it," but that the word itself gives. The word
itself is the giver. What does it give? To go by the poetic
experience and by the most ancient tradition of thinking, the
word gives Being. Our thinking, then, would have to seek
the word, the giver which itself is never given, in this "there
is that which gives."

We are familiar with the expression "there is, there are" in
many usages, such as "There are strawberries on the sunny
slope," *il y a, es gibt,* there are, strawberries; we can find
them as something that is there on the slope. In our present
reflection, the expression is used differently. We do not mean
"There is the word"—we mean "by virtue of the gift of the
word there is, the word gives . . ." The whole spook about
the "givenness" of things, which many people justly fear, is
blown away. But what is memorable remains, indeed it only
now comes to radiant light. This simple, ungraspable situation which we call up with the phrase "it, the word, gives,"
reveals itself as what is properly worthy of thought, but for
whose definition all standards are still lacking in every way.
Perhaps the poet knows them. But his poetry has learned
renunciation, yet has lost nothing by the renunciation. Meanwhile, the prize escapes him nonetheless. Indeed. But it
escapes him in the sense that the word is denied. The denial
is a holding-back. And here precisely it comes to light how
astounding a power the word possesses. The prize does in
no way crumble into a nothing that is good for nothing. The
word does not sink into a flat inability to say. The poet does
not abdicate the word. It is true, the prize does withdraw
into the mysterious wonder that makes us wonder. This is
why, as the preamble to "The song" says, the poet is still
pondering, now even more than before; he is still framing
an utterance, fitting together a saying, otherwise than he did

before. He sings songs. The very first song he sings, and which remains untitled, sings nothing less than the intuited secret of the word, which in denying itself brings near to us its withheld nature. This song sings the word's secret wonderingly, that is, poetically inquiring, in three stanzas of three lines each:

> What bold-easy step
> Walks through the innermost realm
> Of grandame's fairy tale garden?
>
> What rousing call does the bugler's
> Silver horn cast in the tangle
> Of the Saga's deep slumber?
>
> What secret breath
> of yesterday's melancholy
> Seeps into the soul?

Stefan George normally writes all words with small initials, except only those at the beginning of a line.* We notice that in this poem, one single word appears with a capital initial—the word in the last line of the middle stanza: the Saga—Saying. The poet might have called the poem "Saying." He did not do so. The poem sings of the mysterious nearness of the far-tarrying power of the word. Something entirely different is said in the poem in a completely different manner, and yet the Same is said as has been thought earlier concerning the relation of "is" and the word that is no thing.

What about the neighborhood of poetry and thinking? We stand confused between two wholly different kinds of saying. In the poet's song, the word appears as the mysterious wonder. Our thinking reflection of the relation between the "is" and the word that is no thing is faced with something memorable whose features fade into indefiniteness. In the song, wonder appears in a fulfilled, singing saying; in our reflection something memorable appears in a scarcely definable—but certainly not a singing—saying. How can this be a neighborhood, under which poetry and thinking live in close nearness? It

* In standard German usage, all nouns are capitalized. (Tr.)

would seem that the two diverge just as far as can be.

But we should become familiar with the suggestion that the neighborhood of poetry and thinking is concealed within this farthest divergence of their Saying. This divergence is their real face-to-face encounter.

We must discard the view that the neighborhood of poetry and thinking is nothing more than a garrulous cloudy mixture of two kinds of saying in which each makes clumsy borrowings from the other. Here and there it may seem that way. But in truth, poetry and thinking are in virtue of their nature held apart by a delicate yet luminous difference, each held in its own darkness: two parallels, in Greek *para ʾllelo*, by one another, against one another, transcending, surpassing one another each in its fashion. Poetry and thinking are not separated if separation is to mean cut off into a relational void. The parallels intersect in the infinite. There they intersect with a section that they themselves do not make. By this section, they are first cut, engraved into the design of their neighboring nature. That cut assigns poetry and thinking to their nearness to one another. The neighborhood of poetry and thinking is not the result of a process by which poetry and thinking—no one knows from where—first draw near to each other and thus establish a nearness, a neighborhood. The nearness that draws them near is itself the occurrence of appropriation by which poetry and thinking are directed into their proper nature.

But if the nearness of poetry and thinking is one of Saying, then our thinking arrives at the assumption that the occurrence of appropriation acts as that Saying in which language grants its essential nature to us. Its vow is not empty. It has in fact already struck its target—whom else but man? For man is man only because he is granted the promise of language, because he is needful to language, that he may speak it.

III

These three lectures are devoted to an attempt to bring us face to face with a possibility of undergoing an experience with language. The first lecture gives ear to a poetic experience with the word, and traces it in thought. Simply by doing so it moves within the neighborhood of poetry and thinking. There it goes back and forth.

The second lecture reflects on the way of this movement. To the modern mind, whose ideas about everything are punched out in the die presses of technical-scientific calculation, the object of knowledge is part of the method. And method follows what is in fact the utmost corruption and degeneration of a way.

For reflective thinking, on the contrary, the way belongs in what we here call the country or region. Speaking allusively, the country, that which counters, is the clearing that gives free rein, where all that is cleared and freed, and all that conceals itself, together attain the open freedom. The freeing and sheltering character of this region lies in this way-making movement, which yields those ways that belong to the region.

To a thinking so inclined that reaches out sufficiently, the way is that by which we reach—which lets us reach what reaches out for us by touching us, by being our concern.* The way is such, it lets us reach what concerns and summons us. Now it would seem that by thinking in this fashion of what summons us, we manipulate language willfully. Indeed it is willful to gauge the sense in which we here speak of "summoning" by the usual understanding of the word. But the reflective use of language cannot be guided by the common, usual understanding of meanings; rather, it must be guided by the hidden riches that language holds in store for us, so that these riches may summon us for the saying of language.

---

* The following passage, a gloss on the German verb *belangen* (to concern, to summon) and its German cognates, has here been omitted in the translated text: "Wir verstehen freilich das Zeitwort 'belangen' nur in einem gewöhnlichen Sinne, der meint: sich jemanden vornehmen zur Vernehmung, zum Verhör. Wir können aber auch das Be-langen in einem hohen Sinne denken: be-langen, be-rufen, be-hüten, be-halten. Der Be-lang: das, was, nach unserem Wesen auslangend, es verlangt und so gelangen lässt in das, wohin es gehört." (Tr.)

The country offers ways only because it is country. It gives way, moves us. We hear the words "give way" in this sense: to be the original giver and founder of ways.*

The word "way" probably is an ancient primary word that speaks to the reflective mind of man. The key word in Laotse's poetic thinking is *Tao*, which "properly speaking" means way. But because we are prone to think of "way" superficially, as a stretch connecting two places, our word "way" has all too rashly been considered unfit to name what *Tao* says. *Tao* is then translated as reason, mind, *raison*, meaning, *logos*.

Yet *Tao* could be the way that gives all ways, the very source of our power to think what reason, mind, meaning, *logos* properly mean to say—properly, by their proper nature. Perhaps the mystery of mysteries of thoughtful Saying conceals itself in the word "way," *Tao*, if only we will let these names return to what they leave unspoken, if only we are capable of this, to allow them to do so. Perhaps the enigmatic power of today's reign of method also, and indeed preeminently, stems from the fact that the methods, notwithstanding their efficiency, are after all merely the runoff of a great hidden stream which moves all things along and makes way for everything. All is way.

These lectures make their way within the neighborhood of poetry and thinking, underway on the lookout for a possibility of undergoing an experience with language.

On the way, we assume that the neighborhood of which we have spoken is the place that gives us room to experience how matters stand with language. Anything that gives us room and

---

* Again, a passage has been omitted in the translated text—a gloss on the German verb *bewegen* (usually translated "to move"), its German cognates, etymology, and uses in the Swabian dialect. The passage runs: "Sonst verstehen wir bewegen im Sinne von: bewirken, das etwas seinen Ort wechselt, zu- oder abnimmt, überhaupt sich ändert. Be-wëgen aber heisst: die Gegend mit Wegen versehen. Nach altem Sprachgebrauch der schwäbisch-alemannischen Mundart kann "wëgen" besagen: einen Weg bahnen, z. B. durch tief verschneites Land. / Wëgen und Be-wëgen als Weg-bereiten und Weg als das Gelangenlassen gehören in den selben Quell- und Strombereich wie die Zeitwörter: wiegen und wagen und wogen." (Tr.)

allows us to do something gives us a possibility, that is, it gives what enables us. "Possibility" so understood, as what enables, means something else and something more than mere opportunity.

The third lecture intends to bring us properly face to face with a possibility, that is, to enable us to undergo an experience with language. What is necessary here is not only that on our chosen way we stay within the neighborhood of poetry and thinking. We also must look about us in this neighborhood, to see whether and in what manner it shows us something that transforms our relation to language. But of the way which is to lead us to the source of this possibility, it was said that it leads us only to where we already are. The "only" here does not mean a limitation, but rather points to this way's pure simplicity. The way allows us to reach what concerns us, in that domain where we are already staying. Why then, one may ask, still find a way to it? Answer: because where we already are, we are in such a way that at the same time we are not there, because we ourselves have not yet properly reached what concerns our being, not even approached it. The way that lets us reach where we already are, differing from all other ways, calls for an escort that runs far ahead. That escort is implied in the key word which we named in passing at the end of the first lecture. We have not yet commented on this directive character of the guiding key word. Nor could we have done so. For the second lecture had first to direct us straight to the country where the way belongs that is accompanied by the onward-beckoning guide-word. That country makes itself known in the neighborhood of poetry and thinking. Neighborhood means: dwelling in nearness. Poetry and thinking are modes of saying. The nearness that brings poetry and thinking together into neighborhood we call Saying. Here, we assume, is the essential nature of language. "To say," related to the Old Norse "*saga*," means to show: to make appear, set free, that is, to offer and extend what we call World, lighting and concealing it. This lighting and hiding proffer of the world is the essential being of Saying. The guide-word on the way within the neighborhood of poetry and thinking holds an indication which we would follow to come to that nearness by which this neighborhood is defined.

The guide-word runs:

> *The being of language:*
> *The language of being.*

The guide-word holds the primal tidings of linguistic nature. We must now try to hear it more clearly, to make it more indicative of the way that lets us reach what even now reaches and touches us.

The being of language: the language of being.

Two phrases held apart by a colon, each the inversion of the other. If the whole is to be a guide-word, then this colon must indicate that what precedes it opens into what follows it. Within the whole there plays a disclosure and a beckoning that point to something which we, coming from the first turn of phrase, do not suspect in the second; for that second phrase is more than just a rearrangement of the words in the first. If so, then what the words "being" and "language" on either side of the colon say is not only not identical, but even the form of the phrase is different in each case.

An explanation within the scope of grammatical, that is logical and metaphysical, ways of thinking may bring us a little closer to the matter, though it can never do justice to the situation that the guide-word names.

In the phrase before the colon, "the being of language," language is the subject whose being is to be determined. What something is, *to ti estin*, whatness, comprises since Plato what one commonly calls the "nature" or *essentia*, the essence of a thing. Essence so understood becomes restricted to what is later called the concept, the idea or mental representation by means of which we propose to ourselves and grasp what a thing is. Understood less strictly, the phrase before the colon then says: we shall comprehend what language is as soon as we enter into what the colon, so to speak, opens up before us. And that is the language of being. In this phrase being, "essence" assumes the role of the subject that possesses language. However, the word "being" now no longer means what something is. We hear "being" as a verb, as in "being present" and "being absent." "To be" means to perdure and persist. But this says more than just "last and abide." "It is in being" means "it persists in its presence," and in its persistence concerns and moves us. Such being, so conceived, names what persists, what concerns us in all things, because it moves and makes a way for all things. Therefore, the second phrase in the guide-word, "the language of being," says this, that language belongs to this persisting being, is proper to what moves all things because that is its most distinctive property. What moves all things moves in that it speaks. But it remains quite obscure just how we are to think of essential being, wholly obscure how it speaks, and supremely obscure, therefore, what *to speak* means. This is the crux of our reflection on the nature of language. Yet this reflection is already underway along a certain way—the way within the neighborhood of poetry and thinking. The guide-word gives us a hint on this way, but not an answer. But that hint—where does it point? It points only to what defines the neighborhood of poetry and thinking as a neighborhood. Neighborliness, dwelling in nearness, receives its definition from nearness. Poetry and thinking, however, are modes of saying, indeed preeminent modes. If these two modes of saying are to be neighborly in virtue of their nearness, then nearness itself must act in the manner of Saying. Then nearness and Saying would be the Same. The demand to think this is still a flagrant imposition. Its flagrancy must not be softened in the least.

If we were to succeed for once in reaching the place to which the guide-word beckons us, we would arrive where we have a possibility of undergoing an experience with language, the language known to us. Thus, much depends on our keeping to the direction of that indication which the clarified guide-word gives us—this guide-word which we can now paraphrase as follows: what concerns us as language receives its definition from Saying as that which moves all things. A hint beckons away from the one, toward the other. The guide-word beckons us away from the current notions about language, to the experience of language as Saying.

Hints hint in many ways. A hint can give its hint so simply and at the same time so fully that we release ourselves in its direction without equivocation. But it can also give its hint in such a manner that it refers us, from the first and persistently, back to the dubiousness against which it warns us, and lets us only suspect at first the memorable thing toward which it beckons us, as a thought-worthy matter for which the fitting mode of thinking is still lacking. The hint that our guide-word gives is of this kind, for the nature of language is so well known to us through a variety of determinations that we detach ourselves from these only with difficulty. But such detachment must not be forced, because the tradition remains rich in truth. Thus it behooves us first to give thought to our usual notions of language, even if only in their broad outlines, but to do so with forethought to what is indicated by the neighborhood of the two kinds of saying, poetry and thinking: in nearness as Saying. If we take language directly in the sense of something that is present, we encounter it as the act of speaking, the activation of the organs of speech, mouth, lips, tongue. Language manifests itself in speaking, as a phenomenon that occurs in man. The fact that language has long since been experienced, conceived, defined in these terms is attested by the names that the Western languages have given to themselves: *glossa*, *lingua*, *langue*, language. Language is the tongue. The second chapter of the Acts of the Apostles, which tells of the miracle of Pentecost, says in verses 3 and 4:

καὶ ὤφθησαν αὐτοῖς διαμεριζόμεναι γλῶσσαι ὡσεὶ πυρός . . . καὶ ἤρξαντο λαλεῖν ἑτέραις γλώσσαις.

The Vulgate translates: *Et apparuerunt illis dispertitae linguae tamquam ignis . . . et coeperunt loqui variis linguis.* In the Revised Standard Version, the passage runs as follows: "And there appeared to them tongues as of fire, distributed and resting on each one of them. And they . . . began to speak in other tongues. . . ." Yet their speaking is not meant as a mere facility of the tongue, but as filled with the holy spirit, the *pneuma hagion*. Even the biblical idea of language referred to here had been preceded by that Greek description of language of which Aristotle gives the standard formulation. *Logos*, statement, is seen in terms of the phonetic phenomenon of speech. At the beginning of a treatise later entitled *peri hermeneias, De Interpretatione, On Interpretation*, Aristotle says:

> Now, what (takes place) in the making of vocal sounds is a show of what there is in the soul in the way of passions, and what is written is a show of the vocal sounds. And just as writing is not the same among all (men), so also the vocal sounds are not the same. On the other hand, those things of which these (sounds and writings) are a show in the first place, are among all (men) the same passions of the soul, and the matters of which these (the passions) give likening representations are also the same.

These lines of Aristotle constitute the classical passage that allows us to see the structure of which language as vocal sounds is a part: the letters are signs of sounds, the sounds are signs of mental experiences, and these are signs of things. The sign relation constitutes the struts of the structure. We proceed too crudely, though, when we speak everywhere without further definition of signs, of something that signifies and to some extent shows something else. Although Aristotle expressly uses the word *semeia*, signs, he speaks at the same time of *sumbola* and *homoiomata*.

What matters here is that we keep the entire structure of sign relations before our eyes, because it has remained the standard for all later considerations of language, although with numerous modifications.

Language is represented in terms of speech in the sense of vocal sounds. But does not this idea represent a situation in the very nature of language and demonstrable for any language at any time? Certainly. And let no one suppose that we mean to belittle vocal sounds as physical phenomena, the merely sensuous side of language, in favor of what is called the meaning and sense-content of what was said and is esteemed as being of the spirit, the spirit of language. It is much more important to consider whether, in any of the ways of looking at the structure of language we have mentioned, the physical element of language, its vocal and written character, is being adequately experienced; whether it is sufficient to associate sound exclusively with the body understood in physiological terms, and to place it within the metaphysically conceived confines of the sensuous. Vocalization and sounds may no doubt be explained physiologically as a production of sounds. But the question remains whether the real nature of the sounds and tones of speech is thus ever experienced and kept before our eyes. We are instead referred to melody and rhythm in language and thus to the kinship between song and speech. All would be well if only there were not the danger of understanding melody and rhythm also from the perspective of physiology and physics, that is, technologically, calculatingly in the widest sense. No doubt much can be learned this way that is correct, but never, presumably, what is essential. It is just as much a property of language to sound and ring and vibrate, to hover and to tremble, as it is for the spoken words of language to carry a meaning. But our experience of this property is still exceedingly clumsy, because the metaphysical-technological explanation gets everywhere in the way, and keeps us from considering the matter properly. Even the simple fact that we Germans call the different manners of speaking in different sections of the country *Mundarten*, modes of the mouth, hardly ever receives a thought. Those differences do not solely nor primarily grow out of different movement patterns of the organs of speech. The landscape, and that means the earth, speaks in them, differently each time. But the mouth is not merely a kind of organ of the body understood as an organism —body and mouth are part of the earth's flow and growth in which we mortals flourish, and from which we receive the

soundness of our roots. If we lose the earth, of course, we also
lose the roots.

In the fifth stanza of Hölderlin's hymn "Germania," Zeus's
eagle is made to say to "the quietest daughter of God":

> And secretly, while you dreamed, at noon,
> Departing I left a token of friendship,
> The flower of the mouth behind, and lonely you spoke.
> Yet you, the greatly blessed, with the rivers too
> Dispatched a wealth of golden words, and they well
>   unceasing
> Into all regions now.*

Language is the flower of the mouth. In language the earth
blossoms toward the bloom of the sky.

The first stanza of the elegy "Walk in the Country" sings:

> Therefore I even hope it may come to pass,
>   When we begin what we wish for and our tongue loosens,
> And the word has been found and the heart has opened,
>   And from ecstatic brows springs a higher reflection,
> That the sky's blooms may blossom even as do our own,
>   And the luminous sky open to opened eyes.

It must be left to you, my audience, to think about these
verses in the light of what my three lectures are attempting,
so that you may someday see how the nature of language as
Saying, as that which moves all things, here announces itself.
But *one* word that the poet says about the word must not be
passed over—and we will do well to listen now to the gathering of those verses from which that word speaks.

The verses occur at the end of the fifth stanza of the elegy
"Bread and Wine":

> Such is man; when the wealth is there, and no
>   less than a god in
> Person tends him with gifts, blind he remains, unaware.
> First he must suffer; but now he names his most treasured
>   possession,

---

*Translation by Michael Hamburger, *loc. cit.* p. 405. (Tr.)

> Now for it words like flowers leaping alive he
>   must find.*

To think our way through these verses it will be helpful to think over what Hölderlin himself says in another version of this passage, though that will require even deeper reflection:

> Long and hard is the word of this coming but
> White (Light) is the moment. But those who serve the
>   gods know
> The earth well, and their step toward the abyss is
> More human with youth.   but that in the depths is old.**

Once again the word appears in the region, the region that determines earth and sky to be world regions, as it makes earth and sky, the streaming of the deep and the might of the heights, encounter one another. Once again: "words like flowers."

It would mean that we stay bogged down in metaphysics if we were to take the name Hölderlin gives here to "words, like flowers" as being a metaphor.

True, in a curious lecture on "Problems of the Lyric," Gottfried Benn says (1951, p. 16): "This 'like' is always a break in the vision, it adduces, it compares, it is not a primary statement . . . ," it is "a flagging of the tension of language, a weakness of creative transformation." This interpretation may be largely valid, for great and small poets. But it is not valid for Hölderlin's saying, Hölderlin whose poetry Gottfried Benn—correctly from his point of view—regards accordingly as nothing more than a "herbarium," a collection of dried-up plants.

"Words, like flowers": that is not a "break in the vision" but the awakening of the largest view; nothing is "adduced" here, but on the contrary the word is given back into the keeping of the source of its being. There is no lack here of a "primary statement," for here the word is brought forth from its inception; no "weakness of creative transformation" but the

---

*Translation by Michael Hamburger, *loc. cit.* pp. 247/249. (Tr.)
**Cf. Hölderlin, ed. Hellingrath IV, pt. 2, Appendix p. 322. (Tr.)

gentle force of the singular and innocent capacity to hear. A "creative transformation"—the sputnik is that, but it is not a poem. Gottfried Benn, in his own way, has recognized where he himself belongs. He has endured that insight. And this is what gives weight to his poetic work.

When the word is called the mouth's flower and its blossom, we hear the sound of language rising like the earth. From whence? From Saying in which it comes to pass that World is made to appear. The sound rings out in the resounding assembly call which, open to the Open, makes World appear in all things. The sounding of the voice is then no longer only of the order of physical organs. It is released now from the perspective of the physiological-physical explanation in terms of purely phonetic data. The sound of language, its earthyness is held with the harmony that attunes the regions of the world's structure, playing them in chorus. This indication of the sound of speaking and of its source in Saying must at first sound obscure and strange. And yet it points to simple phenomena. We can see them once we pay heed again to the way in which we are everywhere under way within the neighborhood of the modes of Saying. Among these, poetry and thinking have ever been preeminent. Their neighborhood did not come to them by chance, from somewhere or other, as though they, by themselves, could be what they are even away from their neighborhood. This is why we must experience them within, and in terms of, their neighborhood, that is, in terms of what determines that neighborhood to be a neighborhood. Neighborhood, it was said, does not first create nearness; rather, nearness brings about neighborhood. But what does nearness mean?

As soon as we try to reflect on the matter we have already committed ourselves to a long path of thought. At this point, we shall succeed only in taking just a few steps. They do not lead forward but back, back to where we already are. The steps do not form a sequence from here to there, except—at best— in their outward appearance. Rather, they fuse into a concentration upon the selfsame thing, and wend their way back to it. What looks like a digression is in fact the actual proper movement on the way by which the neighborhood is determined. And that is nearness.

When we intend nearness, remoteness comes to the fore. Both stand in a certain contrast to each other, as different magnitudes of our distance from objects. The measurement of magnitude is performed by calculating the length or shortness of intervening stretches. The measurements of the lengths so measured are always taken according to a yardstick by which, along which, the number of units in the measured stretch is counted out. To measure something against something else by moving along it is called in Greek *parametrein*. The stretches along which and past which we measure nearness and remoteness as distances are the temporal sequence of "nows," that is, time; and the spatial side-by-side (beside, in front, behind, above, below) of the points here and there, that is, space. To the calculating mind, space and time appear as parameters for the measurement of nearness and remoteness, and these in turn as static distances. But space and time do not serve only as parameters; in this role, their nature would soon be exhausted—a role whose seminal forms are discernible early in Western thinking, and which then, in the course of the modern age, became established by this way of thinking as the standard conception.

The new theories, that is, methods of space and time measurement, relativity and quantum theories and nuclear physics, have changed nothing in the parametrical character of space and time. Nor can they produce any such change. If they could, then the entire structure of modern technology and natural science would collapse. Nothing today indicates the possibility of such a collapse. Everything argues against it, especially the hunt for the universal mathematical-theoretical formula of the physical world. But the impetus to that hunt does not spring from the personal passion of the investigators. Their nature itself is already of the kind that is driven by a challenge confronting modern thinking as a whole. "Physics and Responsibility"—that is a good thing, and important in today's crisis.

But it remains double-entry accounting, behind which there is concealed a breach that can be cured neither by science nor by morality, if indeed it is curable at all.

However, what has all this to do with the nature of language? More than our thinking can encompass today. We may of course have had an intimation by now, in the form of that positive system which reckons nearness and remoteness as measurements of distance in space and time conceived as parameters.

What is it that here makes us uneasy? The fact that in this way the nearness to which neighborhood belongs can never be experienced. If nearness and neighborliness could be conceived parametrically, then a distance of the magnitude of one millionth of a second, and of one millimeter, would have to mean the nearest possible neighboring nearness, compared with which even the distance of a yard and a minute represents extreme remoteness. Even so, we are bound to insist that a certain spatial-temporal relatedness belongs to every neighborhood. Two isolated farmsteads—if any such are left—separated by an hour's walk across the fields, can be the best of neighbors, while two townhouses, facing each other across the street or even sharing a common wall, know no neighborhood. Neighboring nearness, then, does not depend on spatial-temporal relation. Nearness, then, is by its nature outside and independent of space and time. This view, however, would be premature. We may say only this, that the nearness which prevails in the neighborhood does not depend on space and time considered as parameters. But are time and space something else, then, assuming they *are* at all? Why is it that the parametrical character of space and time prevents neighboring nearness? If we assume that the parameters space and time furnish the standard for neighboring nearness, and thus bring about nearness itself, then they would have to contain even within themselves what distinguishes neighborliness: to be face-to-face with one another. We tend to think of face-to-face encounter exclusively as a relation between human beings. These lectures, too, have indeed restricted face-to-face encounter to the neighborhood of poetry and thinking as modes of saying. We shall for now leave open whether what we have done here is a restriction or a release. Yet being face-to-face with one another has a more distant origin; it originates in that distance where earth and sky, the god and man reach one another. Goethe, and Mörike too, like to use the phrase "face-to-face with one another" not only with respect to human beings but also with respect to things of the world. Where this prevails, all things are open to one another in their self-concealment; thus one extends itself to the other, and thus all remain themselves; one is over the other as its guardian watching over the other, over it as its veil.

In order to experience this face-to-face of things with one another in this way, we must, of course, first rid ourselves of the calculative frame of mind. The movement at the core of the world's four regions, which makes them reach one another and holds them in the nearness of their distance, is nearness itself. This movement is what paves the way for being face-to-face. We shall call nearness in respect of this its movement "nighness." The word seems contrived, but it has grown out of the matter itself in a thinking experience which can be repeated at will; it is no more unlikely than "wilderness" from "wild," or "likeness" from "like." The persisting nature of nearness is not the interstice, but the movement paving the way for the face-to-face of the regions of the world's fourfold. This movement is nearness in the nature of nighness. It remains unapproachable, and is farthest from us whenever we talk "about" it. However, space and time as parameters can neither bring about nor measure nearness. Why not? In the succession of "nows" one after the other as elements of parametric time, one "now" is never in open face-to-face encounter with another. In fact, we may not even say that, in this succession, the "now" coming after and the "now" coming before are closed off from each other. For closure, too, is still a manner of facing or excluding something being in face-to-face. But this encounter is as such excluded from the parametric concept of time.

The same is true of the elements of space; it is true of

numbers of every kind, true of movements in the sense of mathematically calculated spatiotemporal intervals. We conceive of the unbroken and consecutive sequence of parameters, of what is measured by them, as the continuum. It excludes a face-to-face encounter of its elements so resolutely that even where we meet with interruptions, the fractions can never come face-to-face with each other.

Although space and time within their reach as parameters admit of no encounter of their elements, yet the dominance of space and time as parameters for all conceptualization, production, and accumulation—the parameters of the modern technical world—encroaches in an unearthly manner upon the dominion of nearness, that is, upon the nighness of the regions of the world. Where everything is fixed at calculated distances, precisely there, the absence of distance spreads due to the unbounded calculability of everything, and spreads in the form of the refusal of neighborly nearness of the world's regions. In the absence of distance, everything becomes equal and indifferent in consequence of the one will intent upon the uniformly calculated availability of the whole earth. This is why the battle for the dominion of the earth has now entered its decisive phase. The all-out challenge to secure dominion over the earth can be met only by occupying an ultimate position beyond the earth from which to establish control over the earth. The battle for this position, however, is the thoroughgoing calculative conversion of all connections among all things into the calculable absence of distance. This is making a desert of the encounter of the world's fourfold—it is the refusal of nearness. In the battle for dominion over the earth, now, space and time reach their supreme dominion as parameters. However—their power becomes unleashed only because space and time are still, are already, something other than the long-familiar parameters. Their parametrical character obstructs the nature of time and space. Above all it conceals the relation of that nature to the nature of nearness. Simple as these relations are, they remain wholly inaccessible to calculative thinking. Where they are held up to us nonetheless, our current notions resist the insight.

Of time it may be said: time times.

Of space it may be said: space spaces.

The customary notion of time and space takes offense at such talk, and rightly so. For in order to understand it, we need the thinking experience of what is called *identity*.

Time times—which means, time makes ripe, makes rise up and grow. Timely is what has come up in the rising. What is it that time times? That which is simultaneous, which is, that which rises up together with its time. And what is that? We have long known it, only we do not think of it in terms of timing. Time times simultaneously: the has-been, presence, and the present that is waiting for our encounter and is normally called the future. Time in its timing removes us into its threefold simultaneity, moves us thence while holding out to us the disclosure of what is in the same time, the concordant oneness of the has-been, presence, and the present waiting the encounter. In removing us and bringing toward us, time moves on its way what simultaneity yields and throws open to it: time-space. But time itself, in the wholeness of its nature, does not move; it rests in stillness.

The same is to be said about space: it spaces, throws open locality and places, vacates them and at the same time gives them free for all things and receives what is simultaneous as space-time. But space itself, in the wholeness of its nature, does not move; it rests in stillness. Time's removing and bringing to us, and space's throwing open, admitting and releasing—they all belong together in the Same, the play of stillness, something to which we cannot here give further thought. The Same, which holds space and time gathered up in their nature, might be called the free scope, that is, the time-space that gives free scope to all things. Timing and spacing, this Same moves the encounter of the four world regions: earth and sky, god and man—the world play.

The movement of being face-to-face with one another within the world's fourfold generates nearness to its own—it *is* nearness as nighness. Should that movement itself be called the occurrence of stillness?

But what has just now been indicated—does it still say something of the nature of language? It does indeed, even in the same sense as our three lectures have tried to do: to make us face a possibility of undergoing an experience with language, such that our relation to language would in future become memorable, worthy of thought.

Have we now reached such a possibility?

Anticipating, we defined Saying. To say means to show, to make appear, the lighting-concealing-releasing offer of world. Now, nearness manifests itself as the motion in which the world's regions face each other.

There arises the possibility of seeing how Saying, as the being of language, swings back into the presence of nearness. Quiet consideration makes possible an insight into how nearness and Saying, being of the persisting nature of language, are the Same. Language, then, is not a mere human faculty. Its character belongs to the very character of the movement of the face-to-face encounter of the world's four regions.

There arises the possibility that we undergo an experience with language, that we enter into something which bowls us over, that is, transmutes our relation to language. How so?

Language, Saying of the world's fourfold, is no longer only such that we speaking human beings are related to it in the sense of a nexus existing between man and language. Language is, as world-moving Saying, the relation of all relations. It relates, maintains, proffers, and enriches the face-to-face encounter of the world's regions, holds and keeps them, in that it holds itself—Saying—in reserve.

Reserving itself in this way, as Saying of the world's fourfold, language concerns us, us who as mortals belong within this fourfold world, us who can speak only as we respond to language.

Mortals are they who can experience death as death. Animals cannot do so. But animals cannot speak either. The essential relation between death and language flashes up before us, but remains still unthought. It can, however, beckon us toward the way in which the nature of language draws us into its concern and so relates us to itself, in case death belongs together with what reaches out for us, touches us. Assuming that the mover which holds the world's four regions in the single nearness of their face-to-face encounter rests in Saying, then only Saying confers what we call by the tiny word "is," and thus say after Saying. Saying releases the "is" into lighted freedom and therewith into the security of its thinkability.

Saying, as the way-making movement of the world's fourfold, gathers all things up into the nearness of face-to-face encounter, and does so soundlessly, as quietly as time times, space spaces, as quietly as the play of time-space is enacted.

The soundless gathering call, by which Saying moves the world-relation on its way, we call the ringing of stillness. It is: the language of being.

In the neighborhood of Stefan George's poem we heard it said:

> Where word breaks off no thing may be.

We remarked that the poem leaves a thought-provoking residue, to wit, the meaning of "a thing *is*." Equally thought-provoking to us became the relation of the word that is sounded, because it is not lacking, to the "is."

Now, thinking within the neighborhood of the poetic word, we may say, as a supposition:

> An "is" arises where the word breaks up.

To break up here means that the sounding word returns into soundlessness, back to whence it was granted: into the ringing of stillness which, as Saying, moves the regions of the world's fourfold into their nearness.

This breaking up of the word is the true step back on the way of thinking.

THE WAY TO LANGUAGE

THE WAY TO LANGUAGE

To begin, we shall listen to some words of Novalis. They occur in a text which he entitled *Monologue*. That title points to the mystery of language: language speaks solely with itself alone. One sentence in Novalis' text runs: "The peculiar property of language, namely that language is concerned exclusively with itself—precisely that is known to no one."

If we understand all that we shall now attempt to say as a sequence of statements about language, it will remain a chain of unverified and scientifically unverifiable propositions. But if, on the contrary, we experience the way to language in the light of what happens with the way itself as we go on, then an intimation may come to us in virtue of which language will henceforth strike us as strange.

The way to language: that sounds as if language were far away from us, some place to which we still have to find our way. But is a way to language really needed? According to an ancient understanding, we ourselves are after all those beings who have the ability to speak and therefore already possess language. Nor is the ability to speak just one among man's many talents, of the same order as the others. The ability to speak is what marks man as man. This mark contains the design of his being. Man would not be man if it were denied him to speak unceasingly, from everywhere and every which way, in many variations, and to speak in terms of an "it is" that most often remains unspoken. Language, in granting all this to man, is the foundation of human being.

We are, then, within language and with language before all else. A way to language is not needed. Besides, the way to language is impossible if we indeed are already at that point to which the way is to take us. But are we at that point? Are we so fully within language that we experience its nature, that we think speech as speech by grasping its idiom in listening to it? Do we in fact already live close to language even without our doing? Or is the way to language as language the longest road our thinking can follow? Not just the longest, but a way lined with obstacles that come from language itself, as soon as our reflection tries to pursue language straight into its own, without ever losing sight of it?

We are here undertaking something very unusual, which we might paraphrase as follows: we try to speak about speech *qua* speech. That sounds like a formula. It is intended to serve us as a guideline on our way to language. The words "speak, speech" are used three times in the formula, saying something different each time and yet the Same. It is this underlying Same which, in terms of the oneness that is the distinctive property of language, holds together what is kept separate in the formula. To begin with, though, the formula points to a web of relations in which we ourselves are included. The undertaking of a way to speech is woven into a kind of speaking which intends to uncover speech itself in order to present it as speech and to put it into words in the presentation—which is also evidence that language itself has woven us into the speaking.

This web indicated by the formula designates the pre-determined realm in which not only this lecture series but all linguistic science, all linguistic theory and philosophy of language, in fact any attempt to reflect on language, must live.

A web compresses, narrows, and obstructs the straight clear view inside its mesh. At the same time, however, the web of which the guiding formula speaks is the proper matter of language. Therefore, we may not disregard the web which seems to crowd everything into a hopeless tangle. Rather, the formula is to urge our reflection to attempt, not to remove the web, of course, but to loosen it so that it allows us a view into the open togetherness of the relations named in the formula. Perhaps there is a bond running through the web which, in a way that remains strange, unbinds and delivers language into its own. The point is to experience the unbinding bond within the web of language.

The lecture in this series which considers language as information,* and in the process has to consider information as language, refers to this involuted relation as a circle—an unavoidable yet meaningful circle. The circle is a special case of our web of language. It is meaningful, because the direction and manner of the circling motion are determined by language itself, by a movement within language. We might learn the character and scope of this movement from language itself, by entering the web.

How can that be done? By pursuing relentlessly what the guiding formula points to: To speak about speech *qua* speech.

The more clearly language shows itself in its own character as we proceed, the more significant does the way to language become for language itself, and the more decisively does the meaning of our guiding formula change. It ceases to be a formula, and unexpectedly becomes a soundless echo which lets us hear something of the proper character of language.

I

Language: what we have in mind is speaking, which is something we do and are confident of being able to do. Even

*In the series of which this essay originally was a part, C. F. von Weizsäcker spoke on the topic "Language as Information."

so, the power of speech is not a secure possession. Speech may fail a man when he is stunned or terrified. He stands there, struck—and nothing else. He does no longer speak: he is silent. Or a man may lose the power of speech in an accident. He does no longer speak. Nor is he silent. He remains mute. Speaking implies the making of articulated sounds, whether we make them (in speaking), or refrain from making them (in silence), or are incapable of making them (in loss of speech). Speaking implies the articulate vocal production of sound. Language manifests itself in speaking as the activation of the organs of speech—mouth, lips, teeth, tongue, larynx. The names by which language has called itself in the Western languages—*glossa, lingua, langue,* language—are evidence that language has since ancient times been conceived in terms of these phenomena. Language is the tongue, the "lingo."

At the beginning of a treatise later to be titled *peri hermeneias,* "On Interpretation," Aristotle says:

Ἔστι μὲν οὖν τὰ ἐν τῇ φωνῇ τῶν ἐν τῃ ψυχῇ παθημάτων σύμβολα, καὶ τὰ γραφόμενα τῶν ἐν τῃ φωνῇ. καὶ ὥσπερ οὐδὲ γράμματα πᾶσι τὰ αὐτά, οὐδὲ φωναὶ αἱ αὐταί· ὧν μέντοι ταῦτα σημεῖα πρώτων, ταὐτὰ πᾶσι παθήματα τῆς ψυχῆς, καὶ ὧν ταῦτα ὁμοιώματα πράγματα ἤδη ταῦτα.

Only a careful exegesis would permit an adequate translation of this text. Here we shall be content with a makeshift. Aristotle says:

Now, what (takes place) in the making of vocal sounds is a show of what there is in the soul in the way of passions, and what is written is a show of the vocal sounds. And just as writing is not the same among all (men), so also the vocal sounds are not the same. On the other hand, those things of which these (sounds and writings) are a show in the first place, are among all (men) the same passions of the soul, and the matters of which these (the passions) give likening representations are also the same.

Our translation understands *semeia* (that which shows),

symbola (that which holds to each other), and *homoiomata* (that which likens) consistently in terms of showing, in the sense of bringing about the appearance, which in its turn consists in the prevalence of unconcealment (*aletheia*). But our translation disregards the different ways of showing that are mentioned in the text.

Aristotle's text has the detached and sober diction that exhibits the classical architectonic structure in which language, as speaking, remains secure. The letters show the sounds. The sounds show the passions in the soul, and the passions in the soul show the matters that arouse them.

Showing is what forms and upholds the intertwining braces of the architectonic structure. In various ways, disclosing or disguising, Showing makes something come to light, lets what has come to light be perceived, and lets the perception be examined. The kinship of Showing with what it shows—a kinship never developed purely in its own terms and those of its origins—later becomes transformed into a conventional relation between a sign and its signification. The Greeks of the Classical Age know and understand the sign in terms of showing—the sign is shaped to show. Since Hellenistic times (the Stoa), the sign originates by a stipulation, as the instrument for a manner of designation by which man's mind is reset and directed from one object to another object. Designation is no longer a showing in the sense of bringing something to light. The transformation of the sign from something that shows to something that designates has its roots in the change of the nature of truth.*

Since the Greeks, beings are experienced to be whatever is present. Since language *is,* it—whatever speaking occurs at any time—belongs to what is present. Language is represented in terms of speech, in respect of its articulated sounds, carriers of meanings. Speaking is one kind of human activity.

This notion of language, here touched upon only in passing, has in many variant forms remained basic and predominant

---

*See my *Platon's Lehre von der Wahrheit,* 1947. (M. H.)

through all the centuries of Western-European thinking. Though it had its beginnings in Greek antiquity, and though the quest for it took many forms, this view of language reaches its peak in Wilhelm von Humboldt's reflections on language, culminating in the great Introduction to his work on the Kavi language of Java. A year after his death, his brother Alexander von Humboldt published that Introduction separately under the title "On the Diversity of the Structure of Human Language and its Influence on the Intellectual Development of Mankind" (Berlin, 1836).* This treatise, in an open and covert *pro* and *con,* has ever since determined the course of all subsequent philology and philosophy of language.

Every member of my audience in this attempt at a lecture series would have to have thought through and have in mind Wilhelm von Humboldt's astounding, obscure, and yet continuously stimulating treatise. Then all of us would have a common vantage point from which to look into language. Such a common vantage point is lacking. We must put up with this lack—but let us not forget it.

According to Wilhelm von Humboldt, "articulated sound" is "the basis and essence of all speech" (p. 44). In Chapter Five of the treatise, Humboldt formulates those statements which are often cited but rarely given thought, specifically given thought to see how they determine Humboldt's *way to language.* These statements run:

> Properly conceived of, language is something persistent and in every instant transitory. Even its maintenance by writing is only an incomplete, mummified preservation, necessary if one is again to render perceptible the living speech concerned. In

*A translation of this work, under the title *Linguistic Variability and Intellectual Development,* trans. George C. Buck and Frithjof A. Raven (*Miami Linguistic Series No. 9*) (Coral Gables, 1970), was being readied for publication when this translation was still in draft form. The courtesy of the publishers, The University of Miami Press, in making page proofs available at an early stage, and giving permission to use the passages which follow, is gratefully acknowledged. All references below are to the Buck & Raven translation. In the German text, Heidegger refers to the E. Wasmuth reprint edition (1936) of von Humboldt's work. (Tr.)

itself language is not work (*ergon*) but an activity (*energeia*).
Its true definition may therefore only be genetic. It is after all
the continual intellectual effort to make the articulated sound
capable of expressing thought. In a rigorous sense, this is the
definition of speech in each given case. Essentially, however,
only the totality of this speaking can be regarded as language.
(p. 27)

Humboldt here says that he finds the essential element of
language in the act of speaking. Does he thereby also say
what speech, looked at in this way, is *qua* speech? Does he make
the act of speaking, taken as language, speak for itself? We
purposely leave these questions unanswered, but observe the
following:

Humboldt conceives of language as a particular "intellectual
effort." Following this view, he looks for that as which language
shows itself—he looks for what language is. This whatness is
called its nature. If we follow up and define the intellectual
effort with respect to its achievement in speech, that nature, so
understood, is bound to stand out more clearly. Yet the
intellect—in Humboldt's sense, too—lives in other activities and
achievements as well. If, however, language is counted as one
of these, then speaking is not experienced in its own terms, in
terms of language, but rather is referred to something else.
Still, this something else remains too important for us to pass
it over in our reflection on language. What activity does
Humboldt have in mind when he conceives of language as an
intellectual effort? A few lines at the beginning of Chapter
Five give the answer:

Language must be regarded not as a dead product of the past
but as a living creation. It must be abstracted from all that it
effects as a designation of comprehended ideas. Furthermore,
we must revert to a more meticulous examination of its origins
and its interaction with intellectual activity. (p. 26)

Humboldt is referring here to the "inner form of language,"
which is described in his Chapter Eight but difficult to define
in his conceptual terms; we might come a little closer to his

meaning by asking: What is speaking as the expression of thought if we think of it in terms of its origin in the inner activity of the spirit? The answer is contained in a sentence in Chapter Seventeen, whose adequate interpretation would require a separate study:

> If in the soul the feeling truly arises that language is not merely a medium of exchange for mutual understanding, but a true *world* which the *intellect* must set between itself and *objects* by the inner labor of its power, then the soul is on the true way toward discovering constantly more in language, and putting constantly more into it. (p. 135) *

According to the tenets of modern idealism, the labor of the spirit is a positing, a setting (thesis). Because the spirit is conceived as subject, and is accordingly represented within the subject-object model, the positing (thesis) must be the synthesis between the subject and its objects. What is so posited affords a view of objects as a whole. That which the power of the subject develops by its labor and sets between itself and the objects, Humboldt calls "a world." In such a "world view," a humanity achieves its self-expression.

But why does Humboldt regard language as a world and world view? Because *his* way to language is defined, not so much in terms of language as language, but rather in terms of an endeavor to offer a historical presentation of man's whole historical-spiritual development in its totality and yet also in its given individuality. In the fragment of an autobiography dating from 1816, Humboldt writes: "What I am striving for is after all precisely this—to understand the world in its individuality and totality."

An understanding of the world with this orientation can draw on many sources, because the self-expressive power of the spirit is active in a variety of ways. Humboldt recognizes and chooses language as one of the chief sources. While language is not, of course, the only form of world view developed by human subjectivity, it is that form to which we must ascribe

---

* The translation of the Humboldt passage given here differs slightly from the Buck & Raven translation. (Tr.)

a special authority in the history of man's development by virtue of its formative power at each given time. The title of the treatise now becomes somewhat clearer as regards Humboldt's way to language.

Humboldt deals with "the diversity of the structure of human language" and deals with it in respect of "its influence on the spiritual development of mankind." Humboldt puts language into language as *one* kind and form of the world view worked out in human subjectivity.

Into what language? Into a series of assertions that speak the language of the metaphysics of his time, a language in which Leibniz' philosophy plays a decisive role. The authority of that philosophy manifests itself most clearly in the fact that Humboldt defines the nature of language as *energeia*, but understands the word in a wholly un-Greek sense—the sense of Leibniz's monadology as the activity of the subject. Humboldt's way to language is turned in the direction of man, and leads through language on to something else: the endeavor to get to the bottom of and to present the spiritual development of the human race.

However, the nature of language conceived in this light does not thereby show also the linguistic nature: the manner in which language has being, that is, abides, that is, remains gathered in what language grants to itself, to its own idiom, as language.

II

When we reflect on language *qua* language, we have abandoned the traditional procedure of language study. We now can no longer look for general notions such as energy, activity, labor, power of the spirit, world view, or expression, under which to subsume language as a special case. Instead of explaining language in terms of one thing or another, and thus running away from it, the way to language intends to let language be experienced as language. In the nature of language, to be sure, language itself is conceptually grasped—but grasped in the grasp of something other than itself. If we attend to language exclusively as language, however, then language requires of us that we first of all put forward everything that belongs to language as language.

Yet it is one thing to coordinate the various things that are manifest in the linguistic nature, and another to focus our eyes upon that which of itself unifies those things, and which imparts its proper unity to the essence of language.

Our way to language will attempt now to follow more strictly the guideline given by the formula: to speak about speech *qua* speech. The point is to approach more closely language's own peculiar character. Here, too, language shows itself first as our way of speaking. We shall for now attend only to such things as, noticed or unnoticed, have and always have had a voice in speaking, always to the same measure.

Speaking must have speakers, but not merely in the same way as an effect must have a cause. Rather, the speakers are present in the way of speaking. Speaking, they are present and together with those with whom they speak, in whose neighborhood they dwell because it is what happens to concern them at the moment. That includes fellow men and things, namely, everything that conditions things and determines men. All this is addressed in word, each in its own way, and therefore spoken about and discussed in such a way that the speakers speak to and with one another and to themselves. All the while, what is spoken remains many-sided. Often it is no more than what has been spoken explicitly, and either fades quickly away or else is somehow preserved. What is spoken can have passed by, but it also can have arrived long ago as that which is granted, by which somebody is addressed.

Everything spoken stems in a variety of ways from the unspoken, whether this be something not yet spoken, or whether it be what must remain unspoken in the sense that it is beyond the reach of speaking. Thus, that which is spoken in various ways begins to appear as if it were cut off from speaking and the speakers, and did not belong to them, while in fact it alone offers to speaking and to the speakers whatever it is they attend to, no matter in what way they stay within what is spoken of the unspoken.

The nature of language exhibits a great diversity of elements and relations. We enumerated them but did not string them together in series. In going through them, that is, in the original count which does not yet reckon with numbers, some kind of belonging together became manifest. The count is a recounting that anticipates the unifying element in the belonging together, yet cannot bring it out and make it appear.

There is a long history to the inability, here come to light, of the vision of thinking to see directly the unifying unity of the being of language. That is why this unity remains without a name. The traditional names for what we have in mind under the rubric "language" indicate this unity always only in terms of one or another of the aspects which the being of language has to offer.

This unity of the being of language for which we are looking we shall call the design. The name demands of us that we see the proper character of the being of language with greater clarity. The "sign" in design (Latin *signum*) is related to *secare*, to cut—as in saw, sector, segment. To design is to cut a trace. Most of us know the word "sign" only in its debased meaning—lines on a surface. But we make a design also when we cut a furrow into the soil to open it to seed and growth. The design is the whole of the traits of that drawing which structures and prevails throughout the open, unlocked freedom of language. The design is the drawing of the being of language, the structure of a show in which are joined the speakers and their speaking: what is spoken and what of it is unspoken in all that is given in the speaking.

Yet the design of language's nature will remain veiled to us even in its approximate outline, as long as we do not properly attend to the sense in which we had already spoken of speaking and what is spoken.

To be sure, speaking is vocalization. Also, it can be considered a human activity. Both are correct views of language as speaking. Both will now be ignored, though we should not forget how long the vocal aspect of language has already been waiting for a fitting definition; for the phonetic-acoustic-physiological explanation of the sounds of language does not know the experience of their origin in ringing stillness, and knows even less how sound is given voice and is defined by that stillness.

But then, in this short account of the nature of language, in what way are we thinking of speech and what is spoken? They reveal themselves even now as that by which and within which something is given voice and language, that is, makes an appearance *insofar as something is said*. To say and to speak are not identical. A man may speak, speak endlessly, and all the time say nothing. Another man may remain silent, not speak at all and yet, without speaking, say a great deal.

But what does "say" mean? In order to find out, we must stay close to what our very language tells us to think when we use the word. "Say" means to show, to let appear, to let be seen and heard.

In pointing out what follows we shall be saying something that is self-evident, and yet hardly a thought has been given to it and all its implications. To speak *to* one another means: to say something, show something to one another, and to entrust one another mutually to what is shown. To speak *with* one another means: to tell of something jointly, to show to one another what that which is claimed in the speaking says in the speaking, and what it, of itself, brings to light. What is unspoken is not merely something that lacks voice, it is what remains unsaid, what is not yet shown, what has not yet reached its appearance. That which must remain wholly unspoken is held back in the unsaid, abides in concealment as unshowable, is mystery. That which is spoken to us speaks as dictum in the sense of something imparted, something whose speaking does not even require to be sounded.

Speaking, *qua* saying something, belongs to the design of the being of language, the design which is pervaded by all the modes of saying and of what is said, in which everything present or absent announces, grants or refuses itself, shows itself or withdraws. This multiform saying from many different sources is the pervasive element in the design of the being of language. With regard to the manifold ties of saying, we shall call the being of language in its totality "Saying"—and confess that even so we still have not caught sight of what unifies those ties.

We have a tendency today to use the word "Saying," like so many other words in our language, mostly in a disparaging sense. Saying is accounted a mere say-so, a rumor unsupported and hence untrustworthy. Here "Saying" is not understood in this sense, nor in its natural, essential sense of *Saga*. Is it used perhaps in the sense of Georg Trakl's line "the venerable saying of the blue source"? In keeping with the most ancient usage of the word we understand saying in terms of showing, pointing out, signaling. Jean Paul called the phenomena of nature "the spiritual pointer" or "spiritual index finger."*

The essential being of language is Saying as Showing. Its showing character is not based on signs of any kind; rather, all signs arise from a showing within whose realm and for whose purposes they can be signs.

In view of the structure of Saying, however, we may not consider showing as exclusively, or even decisively, the property of human activity. Self-showing appearance is the mark of the presence and absence of everything that is present, of every kind and rank. Even when Showing is accomplished by. our human saying, even then this showing, this pointer, is preceded by an indication that it will let itself be shown.

Only when we give thought to our human saying in this light, only then do we arrive at an adequate definition of what is essentially present in all speaking. Speaking is known as the articulated vocalization of thought by means of the organs of speech. But speaking is at the same time also listening. It is the custom to put speaking and listening in opposition: one man speaks, the other listens. But listening accompanies and surrounds not only speaking such as takes place in conversation. The simultaneousness of speaking and listening has a larger meaning. Speaking is of itself a listening. Speaking is listening to the language which we speak. Thus, it is a listening not *while* but *before* we are speaking. This listening to lan-

*"Der geistige Zeigefinger." (Tr.)

guage also comes before all other kinds of listening that we know, in a most inconspicuous manner. We do not merely speak *the* language—we speak *by way of* it. We can do so solely because we always have already listened to the language. What do we hear there? We hear language speaking.

But—does language itself speak? How is it supposed to perform such a feat when obviously it is not equipped with organs of speech? Yet *language* speaks. Language first of all and inherently obeys the essential nature of speaking: it says. Language speaks by saying, this is, by showing. What it says wells up from the formerly spoken and so far still unspoken Saying which pervades the design of language. Language speaks in that it, as showing, reaching into all regions of presences, summons from them whatever is present to appear and to fade. We, accordingly, listen to language in this way, that we let it say its Saying to us. No matter in what way we may listen besides, whenever we are listening to something we are *letting something be said to us,* and all perception and conception is already contained in that act. In our speaking, as a listening to language, we say again the Saying we have heard. We let its soundless voice come to us, and then demand, reach out and call for the sound that is already kept in store for us. By now, perhaps, at least one trait in the design of language may manifest itself more clearly, allowing us to see how language as speaking comes into its own and thus speaks *qua* language.

If speaking, as the listening to language, lets Saying be said to it, this letting can obtain only in so far—and so near—as our own nature has been admitted and entered into Saying. We hear Saying only because we belong within it. Saying grants the hearing, and thus the speaking, of language solely to those who belong within it. Such is the granting that abides in Saying. It allows us to attain the ability to speak. The essence of language is present in Saying as the source of such grant.

And Saying itself? Is it separated from our speaking, something to which we first must build a bridge? Or is Saying the stream of stillness which in forming them joins its own two banks—the Saying and our saying after it? Our customary notions of language hardly reach as far as that. Saying . . . in our attempt to think of the being of language in terms of Saying, do we not run the risk of elevating language into a fantastic, self-sustained being which cannot be encountered anywhere so long as our reflection on language remains sober? For language, after all, remains unmistakably bound up with human speaking. Certainly. But what kind of bond is it? On what grounds and in what way is it binding? Language needs human speaking, and yet it is not merely of the making or at the command of our speech activity. On what does the being of language rest, that is, where is it grounded? Perhaps we are missing the very nature of language when we ask for grounds?

Or could it even be that Saying is itself the abode of rest which grants the quiet of mutual belonging to all that belongs within the structure of the being of language?

Before thinking further in that direction, let us again attend to the way to language. By way of introduction it was pointed out that the more clearly language comes to light as language itself, the more radically the way to it will change. So far, the way has had the character of a progression that leads our reflection in the direction toward language within the curious web of our guiding formula. Taking our cue from Wilhelm von Humboldt and starting with the speaking process, we tried first to form an idea of the nature of language, and then to get to the bottom of it. Thereafter it became necessary to recount all that belongs to the design of the being of language. This reflection brought us to language as Saying.

III

With the account and explication of the being of language as Saying, our way to language has reached language as such, and thus has reached its goal. Reflection has put the way to language behind it. So it seems, and so indeed it is as long as we take the way to language to be the progression of a thinking which reflects on language. In truth, however, our reflection finds that it has come only within sight of the *way to language* it is seeking; it is barely on its traces. For something has meanwhile come to light in the being of language itself which says: within language as Saying there is present something like a way or path.

What is a way? A way allows us to reach something. Saying, if we listen to it, is what allows us to reach the speaking of language.

The way to speaking is present within language itself. The way to language (in the sense of speaking) is language as Saying. The peculiarity of language, accordingly, conceals itself in the way in which Saying allows those who listen to it to reach language. We can be those listeners only insofar as we belong within Saying. The way to speaking begins with the fact that we are allowed to listen and thus to belong to Saying. This belonging contains the actual presence of the way to language. But in what manner is Saying present, that it can let us listen and belong? If the essence of Saying is ever to make itself manifest, then surely it will do so when we attend with greater instancy to what the foregoing explications have offered.

Saying is showing. In everything that speaks to us, in everything that touches us by being spoken and spoken about, in everything that gives itself to us in speaking, or waits for us unspoken, but also in the speaking that we do *ourselves*, there prevails Showing which causes to appear what is present, and to fade from appearance what is absent. Saying is in no way the linguistic expression added to the phenomena after they have appeared—rather, all radiant appearance and all fading away is grounded in the showing Saying. Saying sets all present beings free into their given presence, and brings what is absent into their absence. Saying pervades and structures the openness of that clearing which every appearance must seek out and every disappearance must leave behind, and in which every present or absent being must show, say, announce itself.

Saying is the gathering that joins all appearance of the in itself manifold showing which everywhere lets all that is shown abide within itself.

Where does the showing spring from? The question asks too much, and asks prematurely. It is enough if we heed what it is that stirs and quickens in the showing and bears its quickness out. Here we need not look far. All we need is the plain, sudden, unforgettable and hence forever new look into something which we—even though it is familiar to us—do not even try to know, let alone understand in a fitting manner. This unknown-familiar something, all this pointing of Saying to what is quick and stirring within it, is to all present and absent beings as that first break of dawn with which the changing cycle of day and night first begins to be possible: it is the earliest and most ancient at once. We can do no more than name it, because it will not be discussed, for it is the region of all places, of all time-space-horizons. We shall name it with an ancient word and say:

The moving force in Showing of Saying is Owning. It is what brings all present and absent beings each into their own, from where they show themselves in what they are, and where they abide according to their kind. This owning which brings them there, and which moves Saying as Showing in its showing we call Appropriation. It yields the opening of the clearing in which present beings can persist and from which absent beings can depart while keeping their persistence in the withdrawal. What Appropriation yields through Saying is never the effect of a cause, nor the consequence of an antecedent. The yielding owning, the Appropriation, confers more than any effectuation, making, or founding. What is yielding is Appropriation itself—and nothing else.* That Appropriation, seen as it is shown by Saying, cannot be represented either as an occurrence or a happening—it can only be experienced as the abiding gift yielded by Saying. There is nothing else from which the Appropriation itself could be derived, even less in whose terms it could be explained. The appropriating event is not the outcome (result) of something else, but the giving yield whose giving reach alone is what gives us such things as a "there is," a "there is" of which even Being itself stands in need to come into its own as presence.**

---

* See my *Identity and Difference* (tr. Joan Stambaugh; New York: Harper & Row, 1969), pp. 37 ff. (M.H.)
** See my *Being and Time* (tr. Macquarrie & Robinson; New York: Harper & Row, 1962), p. 255. (M. H.)

Appropriation assembles the design of Saying and unfolds it into the structure of manifold Showing. It is itself the most inconspicuous of inconspicuous phenomena, the simplest of simplicities, the nearest of the near, and the farthest of the far in which we mortals spend our lives.

We can give a name to the appropriation that prevails in Saying: it—Appropriation—appropriates or owns. When we say this, we speak our own appropriate already spoken language. There are some verses by Goethe that use the word "own" in a meaning close to "showing itself" (though not with reference to the nature of language) . Goethe says:

> Caught soon and late in superstition's snare,
> It owns, it shows itself, it says "beware."

Elsewhere we find a variation:

> Name one thing or name a thousand,
> What we covet, what we fear—
> That life owns itself to thanking,
> Is alone what makes it dear.*

Appropriation grants to mortals their abode within their nature, so that they may be capable of being those who speak. If we understand "law" as the gathering that lays down that which causes all beings to be present in their own, in what is appropriate for them, then Appropriation is the plainest and most gentle of all laws, even more gentle than what Adalbert Stifter saw as the "gentle law." Appropriation, though, is not law in the sense of a norm which hangs over our heads somewhere, it is not an ordinance which orders and regulates a course of events:

Appropriation is *the* law because it gathers mortals into the

---

*Von Aberglauben früh und spat umgarnt:
  Es eignet sich, es zeigt sich an, es warnt.
              (*Faust*, Part II, Act V, "Midnight")

Sei auch noch so viel bezeichnet,
Was man fuerchtet, was begehrt,
Nur weil es dem Dank sich eignet,
Ist das Leben schätzenswert.
              (To the Grand Duke Karl August for New Year 1828)

appropriateness of their nature and there holds them.

Because showing of Saying is appropriating, therefore the ability to listen to Saying—our belonging to it—also lies in Appropriation. In order to grasp this fact and all it implies, we would need to think through the nature of mortals with sufficient completeness in all its respects and rapports, but first of all to think through Appropriation as such.* Here, a suggestion must suffice.

Appropriation, in beholding human nature, makes mortals appropriate for that which avows itself from everywhere to man in Saying, which points toward the concealed. Man's, the listener's, being made appropriate for Saying, has this distinguishing character, that it releases human nature into its own, but only in order that man as he who speaks, that is, he who says, may encounter and answer Saying, in virtue of what is his property. It is: the sounding of the word. The encountering saying of mortals is answering. Every spoken word is already an answer: counter-saying, coming to the encounter, listening Saying. When mortals are made appropriate for Saying, human nature is released into that needfulness out of which man is used for bringing soundless Saying to the sound of language.

Appropriation, needing and using man's appropriations, allows Saying to reach speech. The way to language belongs to Saying determined by Appropriation. Within this way, which belongs to the reality of language, the peculiar property of language is concealed. The way is appropriating.

To clear a way, for instance across a snow-covered field, is in the Alemannic-Swabian dialect still called *wëgen* even today.

---

*Compare *Vorträge und Aufsätze* (1954): "Das Ding" p. 163 ff.; "Bauen Wohnen Denken" p. 145 ff.; "Die Frage nach der Technik" p. 13 ff.—Today, when so much thoughtless and half-thought matter is rushed into print any which way, it may seem incredible to many of my readers that I have used the word "appropriation" (*Ereignis*) in my manuscripts for more than twenty-five years to indicate what is here in my thoughts. The matter, while simple in itself, still remains difficult to think, because thinking must first overcome the habit of yielding to the view that we are thinking here of "Being" as appropriation. But appropriation is different in nature, because it is richer than any conceivable definition of Being. Being, however, in respect of its essential origin, can be thought of in terms of appropriation. (M. H.)

This verb, used transitively, means: to form a way and, forming it, to keep it ready. Way-making understood in this sense no longer means to move something up or down a path that is already there. It means to bring the way . . . forth first of all, and thus to *be* the way.

Appropriation appropriates man to its own usage. Showing as appropriating thus transpires and Appropriation is the way-making for Saying to come into language.

This way-making puts language (the essence of language) as language (Saying) into language (into the sounded word). When we speak of the way to language now, we no longer mean only or primarily the progression of our thinking as it reflects on language. The way to language has become transformed along the way. From human activity it has shifted to the appropriating nature of language. But it is only to us and only with regard to ourselves that the change of the way to language appears as a shift which has taken place only now. In truth, the way to language has its unique region within the essence of language itself. But this means also: the way to language as we first had it in mind does not become invalid; it becomes possible and necessary only in virtue of the true way which is the appropriating, needful way-making. For, since the being of language, as Saying that shows, rests on Appropriation which makes us humans over to the releasement in which we can listen freely, therefore the way-making of Saying into speech first opens up for us the paths along which our thinking can pursue the authentic way to language.

The formula for the way: to speak about speech *qua* speech, no longer merely contains a directive for us who are thinking about language, but says the *forma,* the *Gestalt,* in which the essence of language that rests in Appropriation makes its way.

If we attend without further thought only to the words of our formula, it expresses a mesh of relations in which language becomes entangled. It looks as if any attempt to form a notion of language required dialectical tricks to escape from this tangle. Yet such a procedure, which the formula seems literally to invite, loses the possibility of grasping the simplicity of the essence of language thoughtfully (that is, by entering idiomatically into the way-making movement), instead of trying to form a notion of language.

What looks like a confused tangle becomes untangled when we see it in the light of the way-making movement, and resolves into the release brought about by the way-making movement disclosed in Saying. That movement delivers Saying to speech. Saying keeps the way open along which speaking, as listening, catches from Saying what is to be said, and raises what it thus has caught and received into the sounding word. The way-making of Saying into spoken language is the delivering bond that binds by appropriating.

Language, thus delivered into its own freedom, can be concerned solely with itself. This sounds as if we were talking of a selfish solipsism. But language does not insist upon itself alone in the sense of a purely self-seeking, all-oblivious self-admiration. As Saying, the nature of language is the appropriating showing which disregards precisely itself, in order to free that which is shown, to its authentic appearance.

Language, which speaks by saying, is concerned that our speaking, in listening to the unspoken, corresponds to what is said. Thus silence, too, which is often regarded as the source of speaking, is itself already a corresponding.* Silence corresponds to the soundless tolling of the stillness of appropriating-showing Saying. As Showing, Saying, which consists in Appropriation, is the most proper mode of Appropriating. Appropriation is by way of saying. Accordingly, language always speaks according to the mode in which the Appropriation as such reveals itself or withdraws. For a thinking that pursues the *Appropriation* can still only surmise it, and yet can experience it even now in the *nature* of modern technology, which we call by the still strange-sounding name of Framing (*Ge-Stell***). Because Framing challenges man, that is, provokes him to order and set up all that is present being as technical inventory, Framing persists after the manner of Appropriation, specifically by simultaneously obstructing

* See *Being and Time*, pp. 203-11. (M. H.)
** See *Identity and Difference*, pp. 14n. (M. H.)

Appropriation, in that all ordering finds itself channeled into calculative thinking and therefore speaks the language of Framing. Speaking is challenged to correspond in every respect to Framing in which all present beings can be commandeered.

Within Framing, speaking turns into information.* It informs itself about itself in order to safeguard its own procedures by information theories. Framing—the nature of modern technology holding sway in all directions—commandeers for its purposes a formalized language, the kind of communication which "informs" man uniformly, that is, gives him the form in which he is fitted into the technological-calculative universe, and gradually abandons "natural language." Even when information theory has to admit that formalized language must in the end always refer back to "natural language," in order to put into speech the Saying of the technological inventory by means of nonformalized language, even this situation signifies only a preliminary stage in the current self-interpretation of information theory. For the "natural language" of which one must talk in this context is posited in advance as a not-yet-formalized language that is being set up to be framed in formalization. Formalization, the calculated availability of Saying, is the goal and the norm. The "natural" aspect of language, which the will to formalization still seems forced to concede for the time being, is not experienced and understood in the light of the originary nature of language. That nature is *physis*, which in its turn is based on the appropriation from which Saying arises to move. Information theory conceives of the natural aspect of language as a lack of formalization.

But even if a long way could lead to the insight that the nature of language can never be dissolved in formalism to become a part of its calculations, so that we accordingly must say that "natural language" is language which *cannot be* formalized—even then "natural language" is still being defined only negatively, that is, set off against the possibility or impossibility of formalization.

But what if "natural language," which in the eyes of information theory is no more than a troublesome residue, were

* See *Hebel der Hausfreund* (1957), pp. 34 ff. (M. H.)

drawing its nature, that is, the persistent nature of the being of language, from Saying? What if Saying, instead of merely impeding the destructiveness of information-language, had already overtaken it in virtue of the fact that Appropriation cannot be commandeered? What if Appropriation—no one knows when or how—were to become an insight whose illuminating lightening flash enters into what is and what is taken to be? What if Appropriation, by its entry, were to remove everything that is in present being from its subjection to a commandeering order and bring it back into its own?

All human language is appropriated in Saying and as such is in the strict sense of the word true language—though its nearness to Appropriation may vary by various standards. All true language, because assigned, sent, destined to man by the way-making movement of Saying, is in the nature of destiny.

There is no such thing as a natural language that would be the language of a human nature occurring of itself, without a destiny. All language is historical, even where man does not know history in the modern European sense. Even language as information is not language *per se*, but historical in the sense and the limits of the present era, an era that begins nothing new but only carries the old, already outlined aspects of the modern age to their extreme.

The origin of the word—that is, of human speaking in terms of Saying—its origin which is in the nature of Appropriation, is what constitutes the peculiar character of language.

We recall at the end, as we did in the beginning, the words of Novalis: "The peculiar property of language, namely that language is concerned exclusively with itself—precisely that is known to no one." Novalis understands that peculiarity in the meaning of the particularity which distinguishes language. In the experience of the nature of language, whose showing resides in Appropriation, the peculiar *property* comes close to *owning* and *appropriating*. Here the peculiar property of language receives the original charter of its destined determination, something we cannot pursue here.

The peculiar property of language, which is determined by Appropriation, is even less knowable than the particularity of language, if to know means to have seen something in the wholeness of its nature, seen it in the round. We are not capable of seeing the nature of language in the round because we, who can only say something by saying it after Saying, belong ourselves within Saying. The monologue character of the nature of language finds its structure in the disclosing design of Saying. That design does not and cannot coincide with the *monologue* of which Novalis is thinking, because Novalis understands language dialectically, in terms of subjectivity, that is, within the horizon of absolute idealism.

But language *is* monologue. This now says two things: it is language *alone* which speaks authentically; and, language speaks *lonesomely*. Yet only he can be lonesome who is not alone, if "not alone" means not apart, singular, without any rapports. But it is precisely the absence in the lonesome of something in common which persists as the most binding bond *with* it. The "some" in lonesome is the Gothic *sama*, the Greek *hama*, and the English *same*. "Lonesome" means: the same in what unites that which belongs together. Saying that shows makes the way for language to reach human speaking. Saying is in need of being voiced in the word. But man is capable of speaking only insofar as he, belonging to Saying, listens to Saying, so that in resaying it he may be able to say a word. That needed usage and this resaying lie in that absence of something in common which is neither a mere defect nor indeed anything negative at all.

In order to be who we are, we human beings remain committed to and within the being of language, and can never step out of it and look at it from somewhere else. Thus we always see the nature of language only to the extent to which language itself has us in view, has appropriated us to itself. That we cannot know the nature of language—know it according to the traditional concept of knowledge defined in terms of cognition as representation—is not a defect, however, but rather an advantage by which we are favored with a special realm, that realm where we, who are needed and used to speak language, dwell as *mortals*.

Saying will not let itself be captured in any statement. It

demands of us that we achieve by silence the appropriating, initiating movement within the being of language—and do so without talking about silence.

Saying, which resides in Appropriation, is *qua* showing the most appropriate mode of appropriating. This sounds like a statement. If we hear only this statement, it does not say to us what is to be thought out. Saying is the mode in which Appropriation speaks: mode not so much in the sense of *modus* or fashion, but as the melodic mode, the song which says something in its singing. For appropriating Saying brings to light all present beings in terms of their properties—it lauds, that is, allows them into their own, their nature. Hölderlin sings these words in the beginning of the eighth stanza of "Celebration of Peace":

> Much, from the morning onwards,
> Since we have been a discourse and have heard from one another
> Has human kind learnt; but soon we shall be song.*

Language has been called "the house of Being."** It is the keeper of being present, in that its coming to light remains entrusted to the appropriating show of Saying. Language is the house of Being because language, as Saying, is the mode of Appropriation.

In order to pursue in thought the being of language and to say of it what is its own, a transformation of language is needed which we can neither compel nor invent. This transformation does not result from the procurement of newly formed words and phrases. It touches on our relation to language, which is determined by destiny: whether and in what way the nature of language, as the arch-tidings of Appropriation, will retain us in Appropriation. For that appropriating, holding, self-retaining is the relation of all relations. Thus *our* saying—always an answering—remains forever relational. Relation is thought of here always in terms of the appropriation, and no longer conceived in the form of a mere reference. Our relation

---

*Friedrich Hölderlin, *Poems and Fragments* (Michael Hamburger; Ann Arbor: University of Michigan Press, 1967), p. 438. (Tr.)
**In Heidegger, *Letter on Humanism*, 1947. (Tr.)

to language defines itself in terms of the mode in which we, who are needed in the usage of language, belong to the Appropriation.

We might perhaps prepare a little for the change in our relation to language. Perhaps this experience might awaken: All reflective thinking is poetic, and all poetry in turn is a kind of thinking. The two belong together by virtue of that Saying which has already bespoken itself to what is unspoken because it is a thought as a thanks.

We know that the possibility of an innate transformation of language entered Wilhelm von Humboldt's sphere of thought, from a passage in his treatise on "The Diversity of the Structure of Human Language." As his brother tells us in the foreword, Humboldt worked on this treatise "lonesome, near a grave" until his death.

Wilhelm von Humboldt, whose deep dark insights into the nature of language we must never cease to admire, says:

> The *application* of an already available phonetic form to the internal purposes of language . . . may be deemed possible in the middle periods of *language development*. A people could, by inner illumination and favorable external circumstances, impart so different a form to the language handed down to them that it would thereby turn into a wholly other, wholly new language.

In a later passage we read:

> Without altering the language as regards its sounds and even less its forms and laws, *time*—by a growing development of ideas, increased capacity for sustained thinking, and a more penetrating sensibility—will often introduce into language what it did not possess before. Then the old shell is filled with a new meaning, the old coinage conveys something different, the old laws of syntax are used to hint at a differently graduated sequence of ideas. All this is a lasting fruit of a people's *literature*, and within literature especially of *poetry* and *philosophy*.*

* The two passages will be found on pp. 55 and 65 of the Buck & Raven translation. The rendering given here follows somewhat more closely the text cited by Heidegger. (Tr.)

WORDS

WORDS

From where we are now, let us for a moment think about what Hölderlin asks in his elegy "Bread and Wine" (stanza vi):

> Why are they silent, too, the theatres ancient and hallowed?
> Why not now does the dance celebrate, consecrate joy?**

The word is withheld from the former place of the gods' appearance, the word as it was once word. How was it then? The approach of the god took place in Saying itself. Saying was in itself the allowing to appear of that which the saying ones saw because it had already looked at them. That look brought the saying and the hearing ones into the un-finite intimacy of the strife between men and gods. However, That which is yet above the gods and men prevailed through this strife—as Antigone says!

> *ou gar ti moi Zeus en, ho keruxas tade,*
>
> (l. 450)

* Translation by Joan Stambaugh.
** Friedrich Hölderlin, *Poems and Fragments* (tr. Michael Hamburger; Ann Arbor: University of Michigan Press, 1967), p. 249.

"It was not Zeus who sent me the message" (but something other, that directing need).

ou gar ti nun ge kachthes, all' aei pote
ze tauta, koudeis oiden ex hotou' phane.

(ll. 456/7)

"Not only today and tomorrow, but ever and ever it" (*ho nomos,* the directing need) "arises and no one has looked upon that place from which it came into radiance."

The poetic word of this kind remains an enigma. Its saying has long since returned to silence. May we dare to think about this enigma? We are already doing enough if we allow ourselves to be told the enigma of the word by poetry itself—in a poem with the title:

WORDS

Wonder or dream from distant land
I carried to my country's strand

And waited till the twilit norn
Had found the name within her bourn—

Then I could grasp it close and strong
It blooms and shines now the front along . . .

Once I returned from happy sail,
I had a prize so rich and frail,

She sought for long and tidings told:
"No like of this these depths enfold."

And straight it vanished from my hand,
The treasure never graced my land . . .

So I renounced and sadly see:
Where word breaks off no thing may be.*

The poem was first published in the 11th and 12th series of *"Blätter für die Kunst"* in 1919. Later (1928) Stefan George included it in the last volume of poems published in his lifetime, called *Das Neue Reich.*

The poem is structured in seven stanzas of two lines each. The final stanza not only concludes the poem, it opens it up

*Tr. Peter Hertz. (J.S.)

at the same time. This is already evident in the fact that only the final stanza explicitly says what is in the title: *Words*. The final stanza reads:

Where word breaks off no thing may be.

One is tempted to turn the final line into a statement with the content: No thing is where the word breaks off. Where something breaks off, there is a break, a breaking off. To do harm to something means to take something away from it, to let something be lacking. "It is lacking" means "it is missing." Where the word is missing, there is no thing.

It is only the word at our disposal which endows the thing with Being.

What are words, that they have such power?

What are things, that they need words in order to be?

What does Being mean here, that it appears like an endowment which is dedicated to the thing from the word?

Questions upon questions. These questions do not immediately arouse our contemplation in the first hearing and reading of the poem. We are much more likely to be enchanted by the first six stanzas, for they tell of the poet's strangely veiled experiences. The final stanza, however, speaks in a more oppressing way. It forces us to the unrest of thought. Only this final stanza makes us hear what, according to the title, is the poetic intent of the whole poem: Words.

Is anything more exciting and more dangerous for the poet than his relation to words? Hardly. Is this relation first created by the poet, or does the word of itself and for itself need poetry, so that only through this need does the poet become who he can be? All of this and much else besides gives food for thought and makes us thoughtful. Still, we hesitate to enter upon such reflection. For it is now supported only by a single verse of the whole poem. What is more, we have changed this final verse into a statement. Of course, this act of change did not come about through sheer willfulness. Rather, we are almost forced to make the change, as soon as we notice that the first line of the final stanza ends with a colon. The colon arouses the expectation that it will be followed by a statement. This is the case in the fifth stanza, too. At the end of the first line of that stanza there is also a colon:

> She sought for long and tidings told:
> "No like of this these depths enfold."

The colon opens something up. What follows speaks, seen grammatically, in the indicative: "No like of this . . ." Furthermore, what the twilit norn says is placed between quotation marks.

The case is different in the final stanza. Here, too, there is a colon at the end of the first line. But what follows the colon neither speaks in the indicative, nor are there quotation marks around what is said. What is the difference between the fifth and the seventh stanza? In the fifth stanza, the twilit norn announces something. The announcement is a kind of statement, a revelation. In contrast, the tone of the final stanza is concentrated in the word "renounce."

Renouncing is not stating, but perhaps after all a Saying. Renouncing belongs to the verb to forgive. Accusing, charging is the same word as showing, Greek *deiknumi,* Latin *dicere.* To accuse, to show means: to allow to be seen, to bring to appearance. This, however, showing and allowing to be seen, is the meaning of the old German word *sagan,* to say. To accuse, to charge someone means: to tell him something straight to his face. Accordingly, Saying dominates in forgiving, in renouncing. How so? Renouncing means: to give up the claim to something, to deny oneself something. Because renouncing is a manner of Saying, it can be introduced in writing by a colon. Yet what follows the colon does not need to be a statement. The colon following the word "renounce" does not disclose something in the sense of a statement or an assertion. Rather, the colon discloses renunciation as Saying of that with which it is involved. With what is it involved? Presumably with that which renunciation renounces.

> So I renounced and sadly see:
> Where word breaks off no thing may be.

But how? Does the poet renounce the fact that no thing may be where the word breaks off? By no means. The poet is so far from renouncing this that he actually assents to what is said. Thus the direction in which the colon discloses renunciation cannot tell of that which the poet renounces. It must rather tell of that with which the poet is involved. But renouncing indisputably means: to deny oneself something. Accordingly, the final verse must, after all, tell of what the poet denies himself. Yes and no.

How are we to think this? The final verse makes us more and more thoughtful and requires us to hear it more clearly as a whole, but to hear the whole as that stanza which at the same time discloses the poem through its conclusion.

> So I renounced and sadly see:
> Where word breaks off no thing may be.

The poet has learned renunciation. To learn means: to become knowing. In Latin, knowing is *qui vidit,* one who has seen, has caught sight of something, and who never again loses sight of what he has caught sight of. To learn means: to attain to such seeing. To this belongs our reaching it; namely on the way, on a journey. To put oneself on a journey, to experience, means to learn.

On what journeys does the poet attain to his renunciation? Through what land do his journeys lead the traveler? How has the poet experienced renunciation? The final stanza gives the directive.

> So I renounced and sadly see:

How? Just as the preceding six stanzas tell of it. Here the poet is speaking of his land. There he is speaking of his journeys. The fourth stanza begins:

> Once I returned from happy sail

"Once" is used here in the old meaning which signifies "one time." In this meaning, it tells of a distinctive time, a unique experience. The telling of the experience, therefore, does not just begin abruptly with the "once." It demarcates itself sharply at the same time from all his other journeys, for the last verse of the immediately preceding third stanza terminates in three dots. The same is true of the last verse of the sixth stanza. Accordingly, the six stanzas which prepare for the seventh, the final stanza, are divided by clear signs into two groups of three stanzas, two triads.

The poet's journeys of which the first triad tells are of a different kind from the sole and unique journey to which the whole second triad is dedicated. In order to be able to contemplate the poet's journeys, particularly the unique one which allows him to experience renunciation, we must first consider the landscape to which the poet's experiencing belongs.

Twice—in the second verse of the first stanza and in the second verse of the sixth stanza, that is, at the beginning and at the end of the two triads—the poet says "my land." The land is his as the assured area of his poetry. What his poetry requires are names. Names for what?

The first verse of the poem gives the answer:

Wonder or dream from distant land

Names for what is borne to the poet from the distance as something full of wonder or for what visits him in dreams. For the poet, both of these mean in all assurance what truly concerns him, that which is. Yet he does not want to keep that which is to himself, but to portray it. In order to do this, names are necessary. They are words by which what already is and is believed to be is made so concrete and full of being that it henceforth shines and blooms and thus reigns as the beautiful everywhere in the land. The names are words that portray. They present what already is to representational thinking. By their power of portrayal the names bear witness to their decisive rule over things. The poet himself composes in virtue of the claim to the names. In order to reach them, he must first in his journeys attain to that place where his claim finds the required fulfillment. This happens at his country's strand. The strand bounds, it arrests, limits and circumscribes the poet's secure sojourn. The bourne, the well from which the twilit norn, the ancient goddess of fate, draws up the names is at the edge of the poet's land—or is the edge itself the well? With these names she gives the poet those words which he, confidently and sure of himself, awaits as the portrayal of what he believes to be that which is. The poet's claim to the rule of his Saying is fulfilled. The flourishing and shining of his poetry become presence. The poet is sure of his word, and just as fully in command of it. The last stanza of the first triad begins with the decisive "then."

> Then I could grasp it full and strong
> It blooms and shines now the front along . . .

Let us pay keen attention to the shift in the tenses of the verbs in the second verse of this stanza as compared with the first. The verbs now speak in the present tense. The rule of poetry is completed. It has reached its goal and is perfected. No lack, no doubt disturbs the poet's self-assurance.

Until a wholly different experience strikes him. It is told in the second triad which is formed in exact correspondence to the first. The characteristics of this correspondence are these: the last stanzas of both triads each begins with temporal indications—"Then," "And straight." A dash at the end of the second verse precedes the "Then." A sign also precedes the "And straight"—the quotation mark in the fifth stanza.

From his unique journey the poet no longer brings "wonder or dream from distant land" to his country's strand. After a good journey he arrives with a treasure at the source of the norn. The treasure's origin remains obscure. The poet simply holds it in his hand. What lies in his hand is neither a dream nor something fetched from a distance. But the strange precious jewel is both "rich and frail." Hence the goddess of fate must search long for the jewel's name and must finally take leave of the poet with the message:

> "No like of this these depths enfold."

The names held in the depths of the well are taken as something slumbering which only needs to be awakened in order to be used for the portrayal of things. The names and words are like a staple supply coordinated with the things and retroactively given them for the portrayal. But this source from which until now poetic Saying took its words—words which as names portrayed that which is—this source no longer bestows anything.

What experience befalls the poet? Only this, that the name never comes for the treasure lying in his hand? Only this, that now the treasure must do without its name, but may otherwise remain in the poet's hand? No. Something else, something disturbing happens. However, neither the absence of the name nor the slipping away of the treasure is what is disturbing. What is disturbing is the fact that *with* the absence of the word, the treasure disappears. Thus, it is the word which first holds the treasure in its presence, indeed first fetches and brings it there and preserves it. Suddenly the word shows a different, a higher rule. It is no longer just a name-giving grasp reaching for what is present and already portrayed, it is not only a means of portraying what lies before us. On the contrary, the word first bestows presence, that is, Being in which things appear as beings.

This different rule of the word glances abruptly at the poet. At the same time, however, the word which thus rules remains absent. Hence the treasure slips away. But it by no means disintegrates into nothingness. It remains a treasure, although the poet may never keep it in his land.

> And straight it vanished from my hand,
> The treasure never graced my land . . .

May we go so far as to think that the poet's journeys to the norn's source have now come to an end? Presumably we may. For by this new experience the poet has caught sight of a different rule of the word, although in a veiled manner. Where does this experience take the poet and his previous poetry? The poet must relinquish the claim to the assurance that he will on demand be supplied with the name for that which he has posited as what truly is. This positing and that claim he must now deny himself. The poet must renounce having words under his control as the portraying names for what is posited. As self-denial, renunciation is a Saying which says to itself:

> Where word breaks off no thing may be.

While we were discussing the first six stanzas and considering what journey allowed the poet to experience his renunciation, the renunciation itself has also become somewhat clearer to us. Only somewhat; for much still remains obscure in this poem, above all the treasure for which the name is denied. This is also the reason why the poet cannot say what this treasure is. We have even less right to conjecture about it than he, unless the poem itself were to give us a hint. It does so. We perceive it if we listen thoughtfully enough. To do so it is enough that we ponder something which must now make us most thoughtful of all.

The insight into the poet's experience with the word, that is, the insight into the renunciation he has learned, compels us to ask the question: why could the poet not renounce Saying, once he had learned renunciation? Why does he tell precisely of renunciation? Why does he go so far as to compose a poem with the title "Words"? Answer: Because this renunciation is a genuine renunciation, not just a rejection of Saying, not a mere lapse into silence. As self-denial, renunciation remains Saying. It thus preserves the relation to the word. But because the word is shown in a different, higher rule, the relation to the word must also undergo a transformation. Saying attains to a different articulation, a different *melos*, a different tone. The poem itself, which tells of renunciation, bears witness to the fact that the poet's renunciation is experienced in this sense— by singing of renunciation. For this poem is a song. It belongs to the last part of the last volume of poems published by Stefan George himself. This last part bears the title "Song," and begins with the prologue:

> What I still ponder and what I still frame,
> What I still love — their features are the same.

Pondering, framing, loving is Saying: a quiet, exuberant bow, a jubilant homage, a eulogy, a praise: *laudare*. *Laudes* is the Latin name for songs. To recite song is: to sing. Singing is the gathering of Saying in song. If we fail to understand the lofty meaning of song as Saying, it becomes the retroactive setting to music of what is spoken and written.

With *Song*, with the last poems collected under this title, the poet definitively leaves the sphere that earlier was his own. Where does he go? To renunciation, which he has learned. This learning was a sudden experience which he had in that instant when the wholly different rule of the word looked at him and disturbed the self-assurance of his earlier Saying. Something undreamed of, something terrifying stared him in the face—that only the word lets a thing be as thing.

From that moment on, the poet must answer to this mystery of the word—the mystery of which he has barely an inkling, and which he can only surmise in his pondering. He can succeed only when the poetic word resounds in the tone of the song. We can hear this tone with particular clarity in one of the songs which, without a title, is published for the first time in the last part of the last book of poems (*Das Neue Reich*, p. 137).

> In the stillest peace
> of a musing day
> Suddenly breaks a sight which
> With undreamed terror
> Troubles the secure soul
>
> As when on the heights
> The solid stem
> Towers motionless in pride
> And then late a storm
> Bends it to the ground:
>
> As when the sea
> With shrill scream
> With wild crash
> Once again thrusts
> Into the long-abandoned shell.

The rhythm of this song is as marvelous as it is clear. It is enough to suggest it with a short remark. Rhythm, *rhusmos,* does not mean flux and flowing, but rather form. Rhythm is what is at rest, what forms the movement of dance and song, and thus lets it rest within itself. Rhythm bestows rest. In the song we just heard, the structure shows itself if we pay heed to the one fugue which sings to us, in three forms, in the three stanzas: secure soul and sudden sight, stem and storm, sea and shell.

But the strange thing about this song is a mark which the poet sets down, the only mark besides the final period. Even stranger is the place where he has put the mark—the colon at the end of the last line of the middle stanza. This mark, in this place, is all the more astonishing because both stanzas, the middle and the last one, begin alike with an *as* that refers back to the first stanza:

> As when on the heights
> The solid stem

and:

> As when the sea
> With shrill scream

Both stanzas appear to be arranged in the same way with regard to their sequence. But they are not. The colon at the end of the middle stanza makes the next and final stanza refer back explicitly to the first stanza, by including the second stanza with the first in its reference. The first stanza speaks of the poet disturbed in his security. But yet the "undreamed terror" does not destroy him. But it does bend him to the ground as the storm bends the tree, so that he may become open for that of which the third stanza sings after the opening colon. Once again the sea thrusts its unfathomable voice into the poet's ears which are called the "long-abandoned shell"; for until now the poet remained without the purely bestowed prevalence of the word. Instead, the names required by the norn nourished the self-assurance of his masterful proclamation.

The renunciation thus learned is no mere refusal of a claim, but rather the transformation of Saying into the echo of an inexpressible Saying whose sound is barely perceptible and songlike. Now we should be in a better position to ponder the last stanza so that it may itself speak in such a way that the whole poem is gathered up in it. If we were to succeed in this even to a small degree, we might, at favorable moments, hear more clearly the title of the poem *Words,* and understand how the final stanza not only concludes the poem, not only reveals it, but how it at the same time conceals the mystery of the word.

> So I renounced and sadly see:
> Where word breaks off no thing may be.

The final stanza speaks of the word in the manner of re-nunciation. Renunciation is in itself a Saying: self-denial . . . namely denying to oneself the claim to something. Understood in this way, renunciation retains a negative character: "no thing," that is, not a thing; "the word breaks off," that is, it is not available. According to the rule, double negation produces an affirmation. Renunciation says: a thing may be only where the word is granted. Renunciation speaks affirmatively. The mere refusal not only does not exhaust the essence of renunci-ation, it does not even contain it. Renunciation does have a negative side, but it has a positive side as well. But to talk about sides here is misleading. In so doing we equate what denies and what affirms and thus obscure what truly rules in Saying. This we must think about above all else. Still more. We need to consider what kind of renunciation the final stanza means. It is unique in its kind, because it isn't related to just any possession of just anything. As self-denial, that is, as Saying, renunciation concerns the word itself. Renunciation gets the relation to the word underway toward that which concerns every Saying as Saying. We suspect that in this self-denial the relation to the word gains a nearly "excessive intimacy." The enigmatic quality of the final stanza grows beyond us. Nor would we want to solve it, that enigmatic quality, but only to read, to gather our thoughts about it.

At first we think renunciation as denying-oneself-something. Grammatically, "oneself" is in the dative case and refers to the poet. What the poet denies himself is in the accusative case. It is the claim to the representational rule of the word. Meanwhile, another characteristic of this renunciation has come to light. Renunciation commits itself to the higher rule of the word which first lets a thing be as thing. The word makes the thing into a thing—it "bethings" the thing. We should like to call this rule of the word "bethinging" (*die Bedingnis*). This old word has disappeared from linguistic usage. Goethe still knew it. In this context, however, bethinging says something different from talking about a condition, which was still Goethe's understanding of bethinging. A condition is the existent ground for something that is. The condition gives reasons, and it grounds. It satisfies the principle of sufficient reason. But the word does not give reasons for the thing. The word allows the thing to presence as thing. We shall call this allowing bethinging. The poet does not explain what this bethinging is. But the poet commits himself, that is, his Saying to this mystery of the word. In such commitment, he who renounces denies himself to the claim which he formerly willed. The meaning of self-denial has been transformed. The "self" is no longer in the dative but the accusative case, and the claim is no longer in the accusative but the dative case. The poet's own transformation is concealed in the transformation of the grammatical meaning of the phrase "to deny the claim to oneself" into "to deny oneself to the claim." He has allowed himself—that is, such Saying as will still be possible for him in the future—to be brought face to face with the word's mystery, the be-thinging of the thing in the word.

However, even in this transformed self-denial, the negative character of renunciation still maintains the upper hand. Yet it became clearer and clearer that the poet's renunciation is in no way a negation, but rather an affirmation. Self-denial—which appears to be only refusal and self-withdrawal—is in truth nondenial of self: to the mystery of the word. This nondenial of self can speak in this way only, that it says: "may there be."

From now on may the word be: the bethinging of the thing.
This "may there be" lets be the relation of word and thing,
what and how it really *is*. Without the word, no thing is. In the
"may there be," renunciation commits itself to the "is." Hence
no retroactive transformation of the final verse into a statement is needed in order to make the "is" appear. "May there
be" extends to us the "is" in a veiled and therefore purer
fashion.

> Where word breaks off no thing may be.

In this nondenial of self, renunciation says itself as that kind
of Saying which owes itself wholly to the mystery of the word.
In nondenial of self, renunciation is an owing of self. Here is
the abode of renunciation. Renunciation owes thanks—it is a
thanking. It is not mere refusal, still less a loss.

But why, then, is the poet sad?

> So I renounced and sadly see:

Is it renunciation that makes him sad? Or did sadness come
over him only when he learned renunciation? In the latter
case, the sadness which recently burdened his spirit could have
disappeared again as soon as he had embraced renunciation as
a thanks; for owing oneself as thanking is attuned to joy. The
tone of joy is heard in another song. That poem, too, is without
a title. But it bears such a strangely unique mark that we are
compelled to listen to it in virtue of its inner kinship to the
song *Words* (*Das Neue Reich*, p. 125). It reads:

> What bold-easy step
> Walks through the innermost realm
> Of grandame's fairytale garden?
>
> What rousing call does the bugler's
> Silver horn cast in the tangle
> Of the Saying's deep slumber?

> What secret breath
> Of melancholy just fled
> Nestles into the soul?

Stefan George is in the habit of writing all words with small
initials* except those at the beginning of the lines. But in this
poem there is a single capitalized word, almost at the center of
the poem at the end of the middle stanza. The word is: Saying.
The poet could have chosen this word for the poem's title, with
the hidden allusion that Saying, as the tale of the fairy tale
garden, tells of the origin of the word.

The first stanza sings of the *step* as the journey through the
realm of Saying. The second stanza sings of the *call* that
awakens Saying. The third stanza sings of the *breath* that
nestles into the soul. Step (that is, way) and call and breath
hover around the rule of the word. Its mystery has not only
disturbed the soul that formerly was secure. It has also taken
away the soul's melancholy which threatened to drag it down.
Thus, sadness has vanished from the poet's relation to the
word. This sadness concerned only his learning of renunciation. All this would be true if sadness were the mere opposite
to joy, if melancholy and sadness were identical.

But the more joyful the joy, the more pure the sadness
slumbering within it. The deeper the sadness, the more summoning the joy resting within it. Sadness and joy play into
each other. The play itself which attunes the two by letting
the remote be near and the near be remote is pain. This is why
both, highest joy and deepest sadness, are painful each in its
way. But pain so touches the spirit of mortals that the spirit
receives its gravity from pain. That gravity keeps mortals with
all their wavering at rest in their being. The spirit which
answers to pain, the spirit attuned by pain and to pain, is
melancholy. It can depress the spirit, but it can also lose its
burdensomeness and let its "secret breath" nestle into the soul,
bestow upon it the jewel which arrays it in the precious relation to the word, and with this raiment shelters it.

This, presumably, is what the third stanza of our last poem

---

* In standard German, all nouns are capitalized. (Tr.)

has in mind. With the secret breath of melancholy just fled, sadness permeates renunciation itself; for sadness belongs to renunciation if we think renunciation in its innermost gravity. That gravity is the nondenial of self to the mystery of the word, to the fact that the word is the bethinging of the thing.

As mystery, the word remains remote. As a mystery that is experienced, the remoteness is near. The perdurance of this remoteness of such nearness is the nondenial of self to the word's mystery. There is no word for this mystery, that is, no Saying which could bring the being of language to language.

The treasure which never graced the poet's land is the word for the being of language. The word's rule and sojourn, abruptly caught sight of, its presencing, would like to enter its own word. But the word for the being of the word is not granted.

What if this, the word for the presencing of language, were alone the treasure which, close to the poet since it lies in his hand, still vanishes and yet, having vanished, never having been captured, still remains what is most remote in the nearest nearness? In this nearness, the treasure is mysteriously familiar to the poet, otherwise he could not sing of it as "rich and frail."

Rich means: capable of bestowing, capable of offering, of allowing to attain and reach. But this is the word's essential richness that in Saying, that is, in showing, it brings the thing as thing to radiance.

Frail means according to the old verb *zarton* the same as: familiar, giving joy, saving. Saving is an offering and a releasing, but without will and force, without addiction and dominance.

The *treasure rich and frail* is the word's hidden essence (verbal) which, invisibly in its Saying and even already in what is unsaid, extends to us the thing as thing.

His renunciation having pledged itself to the word's mystery, the poet retains the treasure in remembrance by renunciation. In this way, the treasure becomes that which the poet—he who says—prefers above all else and reveres above everything else.

The treasure becomes what is truly worthy of the poet's thought. For what could be more worthy of thought for the saying one than the word's being veiling itself, than the fading word for the word?

If we listen to the poem as a song in harmony with kindred songs, we then let the poet tell us, and let ourselves be told together with him, what is worthy of the thinking of poetic being.

To let ourselves be told what is worthy of thinking means— to think.

While listening to the poem, we are pondering poetry. This is how making poetry and thinking *are*.

What at first looks like the title of a thesis—making poetry and thinking—turns out to be the inscription in which our destined human existence has ever been inscribed. The inscription records that poetry and thinking belong together. Their coming together has come about long ago. As we think back to that origin, we come face to face with what is primevally worthy of thought, and which we can never ponder sufficiently. It is the same element worthy of thought that glanced abruptly at the poet and to which he did not deny himself when he said:

> Where word breaks off no thing may be.

The word's rule springs to light as that which makes the thing be a thing. The word begins to shine as the gathering which first brings what presences to its presence.

The oldest word for the rule of the word thus thought, for Saying, is *logos:* Saying which, in showing, lets beings appear in their "it is."

The same word, however, the word for Saying, is also the word for *Being,* that is, for the presencing of beings. Saying and Being, word and thing, belong to each other in a veiled way, a way which has hardly been thought and is not to be thought out to the end.

All essential Saying hearkens back to this veiled mutual belonging of Saying and Being, word and thing. Both poetry

and thinking are distinctive Saying in that they remain delivered over to the mystery of the word as that which is most
worthy of their thinking, and thus ever structured in their
kinship.

In order that we may in our thinking fittingly follow and
lead this element worthy of thought as it gives itself to poetry,
we abandon everything which we have now said to oblivion.
We listen to the poem. We grow still more thoughtful now
regarding the possibility that the more simply the poem sings
in the mode of song, the more readily our hearing may err.

LANGUAGE IN THE POEM

A Discussion on Georg Trakl's Poetic Work

LANGUAGE IN THE POEM

A Discussion on Georg Trakl's Poetic Work

We use the word "discuss" here to mean, first, to point out the proper place or site of something, to situate it, and second, to heed that place or site. The placing and the heeding are both preliminaries of discussion. And yet it will require all our daring to take no more than these preliminary steps in what follows. Our discussion, as befits a thinking way, ends in a question. That question asks for the location of the site.

Our discussion speaks of Georg Trakl only in that it thinks about the site of his poetic work. To an age whose historical, biographical, psychoanalytical, and sociological interest is focused on bare expression, such a procedure must seem patently one-sided, if not wayward. Discussion gives thought to the site.

Originally the word "site" suggests a place in which everything comes together, is concentrated. The site gathers unto itself, supremely and in the extreme. Its gathering power penetrates and pervades everything. The site, the gathering power, gathers in and preserves all it has gathered, not like an encapsulating shell but rather by penetrating with its light all it has gathered, and only thus releasing it into its own nature.

Our task now is to discuss the site that gathers Georg Trakl's poetic Saying into his poetic work—to situate the site of Trakl's work.

Every great poet creates his poetry out of one single poetic statement only. The measure of his greatness is the extent to which he becomes so committed to that singleness that he is able to keep his poetic Saying wholly within it.

The poet's statement remains unspoken. None of his individual poems, nor their totality, says it all. Nonetheless, every poem speaks from the whole of the one single statement, and in each instance says that statement. From the site of the statement there rises the wave that in each instance moves his Saying as poetic saying. But that wave, far from leaving the site behind, in its rise causes all the movement of Saying to flow back to its ever more hidden source. The site of the poetic statement, source of the movement-giving wave, holds within it the hidden nature of what, from a metaphysical-aesthetic point of view, may at first appear to be rhythm.

Since the poet's sole statement always remains in the realm of the unspoken, we can discuss its site only by trying to point to it by means of what the individual poems speak. But to do so, each poem will itself be in need of clarification. Clarification is what brings to its first appearance that purity which shimmers in everything said poetically.

It is easy to see that any right clarification itself already presupposes discussion. The individual poems derive their light and sound only from the poetic site. Conversely, the discussion of the poetic statement must first pass through the precursory clarification of individual poems.

All thinking dialogue with a poet's poetic statement stays within this reciprocity between discussion and clarification.

Only a poetic dialogue with a poet's poetic statement is a true dialogue—the poetic conversation between poets. But it is also possible, and at times indeed necessary, that there be a dialogue between *thinking* and poetry, for this reason: because a distinctive, though in each case different, relation to language is proper to them both.

The dialogue of thinking with poetry aims to call forth the *nature* of language, so that mortals may learn again to live within language.

The dialogue of thinking with poetry is long. It has barely begun. With respect to Trakl's poetic statement, the dialogue requires particular reserve. A thinking dialogue with poetry can serve the poetic statement only indirectly. Thus it is always in danger of interfering with the saying of the statement, instead of allowing it to sing from within its own inner peace.

The discussion of the poetic statement is a thinking dialogue with poetry. It neither expounds a poet's outlook on the world, nor does it take inventory of his workshop. Above all, the discussion of the poetic statement can never be a substitute for or even guide to our listening to the poem. Thinking discussion can at best make our listening thought-provoking and, under the most favorable circumstances, more reflective.

With these reservations in mind, we shall try first to point to the site of the unspoken statement. To do so we must start with the spoken poems. The question still is: with which poems? The fact that every one of Trakl's poems points, with equal steadiness though not uniformly, to the statement's one site, is evidence of the unique harmony of all his poems in the single key of his statement.

But the attempt we shall now make to point out the site of his statement must make do with just a few selected stanzas, lines, and phrases. Our selection will inevitably seem arbitrary. However, it is prompted by our purpose to bring our consideration at once to the site of the statement, almost as if by a sudden leap of insight.

I

One of Trakl's poems says:

Something strange is the soul on the earth.

Before we know what we are doing, we find ourselves through this sentence involved in a common notion. That notion presents the earth to us as earthly in the sense of transitory. The soul, by contrast, is regarded as imperishable, supraterrestrial. Beginning with Plato's doctrine, the soul is part of the suprasensuous. If it appears within the sensible world, it does so only as a castaway. Here on earth the soul is miscast. It does not belong on earth. Here, the soul is something strange. The body is the soul's prison, if nothing worse. The soul, then, apparently has nothing else to look forward to except to leave as soon as possible the sensuous realm which, seen in Platonic terms, has no true being and is merely decay.

And yet—how remarkable: the sentence

> Something strange is the soul on the earth.

speaks from within a poem entitled "Springtime of the Soul" (142).* And there is in that poem not one word about a supraterrestrial home of the immortal soul. The matter gives us food for thought; we will do well to pay heed to the poet's language. The soul: "something strange." Trakl frequently uses the same construction in other poems: "something mortal" (51), "something dark" (72, 164, 170, 187), "something solitary" (72), "something spent" (95), "something sick" (107, 165), "something human" (108), "something pale" (132), "something dead" (165), "something silent" (188). Apart from its varying content, this construction does not always carry the same sense. Something "solitary," "something strange" could mean a singular something that in the given case is "solitary," or by chance is in a special and limited sense "strange." "Something strange" of that sort can be classified as belonging to the order of the strange in general, and can thus be disposed of. So understood, the soul would be merely one instance of strangeness among many.

But what does "strange" mean? By strange we usually understand something that is not familiar, does not appeal to us—

---

* The numbers in parentheses are the page numbers in the volume Georg Trakl, *Die Dichtungen*, published by Otto Müller Verlag, Salzburg, twelfth edition (no date). They differ from those cited in Heidegger's published text, which refers to an earlier edition. (Tr.)

something that is rather a burden and an unease. But the word we are using—the German *"fremd,"* the Old High German *"fram"*—really means: forward to somewhere else, underway toward . . ., onward to the encounter with what is kept in store for it. The strange goes forth, ahead. But it does not roam aimlessly, without any kind of determination. The strange element goes in its search toward the site where it may stay in its wandering. Almost unknown to itself, the "strange" is already following the call that calls it on the way into its own.

The poet calls the soul "something strange on the earth." The earth is that very place which the soul's wandering could not reach so far. The soul only *seeks* the earth; it does not flee from it. This fulfills the soul's being: in her wandering to seek the earth so that she may poetically build and dwell upon it, and thus may be able to save the earth *as* earth. The soul, then, is not by any means first of all soul, and then, besides and for whatever reason, also a stranger who does not belong on earth.

On the contrary, the sentence:

Something strange is the soul on the earth

gives a name to the essential being of what is called soul. The sentence does not predicate something about the soul whose nature is already known, as though the point were merely to make the supplementary statement that the soul had suffered the unfitting and thus strange accident of finding neither refuge nor response on earth. The soul, on the contrary, *qua* soul is fundamentally, by its nature, "something strange on the earth." Thus it is always underway, and in its wandering follows where its nature draws it. We, meanwhile, are pressed by this question: whither has this "something strange," in the sense just made clear, been called to turn its steps? A stanza from the third part of the poem "Sebastian in Dream" (99) gives the answer:

> O how still is a walk down the blue river's bank
> To ponder forgotten things, when in leafy boughs
> The thrush called to a strange thing to go under.

The soul is called to go under. Then it is so after all: the soul is to end its earthly journey and leave the earth behind! Nothing of the sort is said in the verses just quoted. And yet they speak of "going under." Certainly. But the going under of which these verses speak is neither a catastrophe, nor is it a mere withering away in decay. Whatever goes under, going down the blue river,

> Goes down in peace and silence.
> (*Transfigured Autumn*, 30)

Into what peace does it go? The peace of the dead? But of which dead? And into what silence?

> Something strange is the soul on the earth.

The stanza in which this sentence belongs continues:

> . . . Ghostly the twilight dusk
> Bluing above the mishewn forest . . .

Earlier, the sun is mentioned. The stranger's footfall goes away into the dusk. "Dusk" means, first, darkness falling. "Dusk bluing." Is the sunny day's blueness darkening? Does it fade in the evening to give way to night? But dusk is not a mere sinking of the day, the dissolution of its brightness in the gloom of night. Dusk, anyway, does not necessarily mean the twilight of the end. The morning, too, has its twilight. The day rises in twilight. Twilight, then, is also a rising. Twilight dusk blues over the "mishewn," tangled, withered forest. The night's blueness rises, in the evening.

The twilight dusk blues "ghostly." This "ghostliness" is what marks the dusk. We must give thought to what this oft-named "ghostliness" means. The twilight dusk is the sun's descending course. That implies: twilight dusk is the decline both of the day and of the year. The last stanza of a poem called "Summer's End" (163) sings:

> So quiet has the green summer grown
> And through the silvery night there rings
> The footfall of the stranger.
> Would that the blue wild game were to recall his paths,

> The music of his ghostly years!

These words, "so quiet," recur in Trakl's poetry again and again. One might think that "quiet" means at most a barely audible sound. So understood, what was said refers to our perception. However, "quiet" means slow, slowly fading away. Quiet is what slips away. Summer slips away into autumn, the evening of the year.

> . . . through the silvery night there rings
> the footfall of the stranger.

Who is this stranger? Whose paths are they that a "blue wild game" is to recall? To recall means to "ponder forgotten things,"

> . . . when in leafy boughs
> The thrush called to a strange thing to go under.

In what sense is the "blue wild game" (cf. 73, 139) to recall what is going under? Does the wild game receive its blue from the "blueness" of the "ghostly twilight dusk" which rises as night? The night is dark, to be sure. But darkness is not necessarily gloom. In another poem (133) night is apostrophized with these words:

> O gentle corn flower sheaf of night.

Night is a cornflower sheaf, a gentle sheaf. So, too, the blue game is called "shy game" (98), the "gentle animal" (91). The sheaf of blueness gathers the depth of the holy in the depths of its bond. The holy shines out of the blueness, even while veiling itself in the dark of that blueness. The holy withholds in withdrawing. The holy bestows its arrival by reserving itself in its withholding withdrawal. Clarity sheltered in the dark is blueness. "Clear" originally means clear sound, the sound that calls out of the shelter of stillness, and so becomes clear. Blueness resounds in its clarity, ringing. In its resounding clarity shines the blue's darkness.

The stranger's footfalls sound through the silvery gleam and ringing of night. Another poem (98) says:

And in holy blueness shining footfalls ring forth.

Elsewhere it is said of blueness (104):

. . . the holiness of blue flowers . . . moves the beholder.

Another poem says (79):

. . . Animal face
Freezes with blueness, with its holiness.

Blue is not an image to indicate the sense of the holy. Blueness itself is the holy, in virtue of its gathering depth which shines forth only as it veils itself. Face to face with blueness, brought up short by sheer blueness, the animal face freezes and transforms itself into the countenance of the wild game.

The frozen rigor of the animal face is not the rigor of the dead. As it freezes, the startled animal face contracts. Its gaze gathers so that, checking its course, it may look toward the holy, into the "mirror of truth" (79). To look means here to enter into silence.

Mighty the power of silence in the rock

runs the next line. The rock is the mountain sheltering pain. The stones gather within their stony shelter the soothing power, pain stilling us toward essential being. Pain is still "with blueness." Face to face with blueness, the wild game's face retracts into gentleness. Gentleness transmutes discord by absorbing the wounding and searing wildness into appeased pain.

Who is this blue wild game to whom the poet calls out that it recall the stranger? Is it an animal? No doubt. Is it just an animal? No. For it is called on to recall, to think. Its face is to look our for . . ., and to look on the stranger. The blue game is an animal whose animality presumably does not consist in its animal nature, but in that thoughtfully recalling look for which the poet calls. This animality is still far away, and barely to be seen. The animality of the animal here intended thus vacillates in the indefinite. It has not yet been gathered up into its essential being. This animal—the thinking animal, *animal rationale,* man—is, as Nietzsche said, not yet determined.

This statement does not mean at all that man has not yet been "confirmed" as a *factum.* On the contrary, he is all too firmly confirmed as a *factum.* The word means: this animal's animality has not yet been gathered up onto firm ground, that is to say, has not been gathered "home," into its own, the home of its veiled being. This definition is what Western-European metaphysics has been struggling to achieve ever since Plato. It may be struggling in vain. It may be that its way into the "underway" is still blocked. This animal not yet determined in its nature is modern man.

By the poetic name "blue wild game" Trakl evokes that human nature whose countenance, whose countering glance, is sighted by the night's blueness, as it is thinking of the stranger's footfalls and thus is illumined by the holy. The name "blue game" names mortals who would think of the stranger and wander with him to the native home of human being.

Who are they that begin such a journey? Presumably they are few, and unknown, since what is of the essence comes to pass in quiet, and suddenly, and rarely. The poet speaks of such wanderers in the second stanza of his poem "Winter Evening" (120) which begins:

> Many a man in his wanderings
> Comes to the gate by darksome paths.

The blue game, where and when it is in being, has left the previous form of man's nature behind. Previous man decays in that he loses his being, which is to say, decays.

Trakl calls one of his poems "Seven-Song of Death." Seven is the holy number. The song sings of the holiness of death. Death is not understood here vaguely, broadly, as the conclusion of earthly life. "Death" here means poetically the "going down" to which "something strange" is being called. This is why the "something strange" that is being called is also referred to as "something dead" (134). Its death is not decay, but that

it leaves behind the form of man which has decayed. Accordingly, the second stanza from the end of "Seven-Song of Death"
(134) says:

> O man's decomposed form: joined of cold metals,
> Night and terror of sunken forests,
> And the animal's searing wildness;
> Windless lull of the soul.

Man's decomposed form is abandoned to searing torture and
pricking thorns. Blueness does not irradiate its wildness. The
soul of this human form is not fanned by the wind of the holy.
And so, it has no course. The wind itself, God's wind, thus
remains solitary. A poem speaking of blue wild game—which,
however, can as yet barely extricate themselves from the
"thicket of thorns"—closes with the lines (93):

> There always sings
> Upon black walls God's solitary wind.

"Always" means: as long as the year and its solar course
remain in the gloom of winter and no one thinks of the path
on which the stranger with "ringing footfalls" walks through
the night. The night is itself only the sheltering veiling of the
sun's course. "Walk," *ienai,* is the Indogermanic *ier,* the year.

> Would that the blue wild game were to recall his paths,
>
> The music of his ghostly years!

The year's ghostliness is defined by the ghostly twilight of
the night.

> O how earnest the hyacinthine face of the twilight.
>   (*Wayfaring*, 96)

The ghostly twilight is of so essential a nature that the poet
gave to one of his poems the specific title "Ghostly Twilight"
(131). In that poem, too, wild game is met, but this game is
dark. Its wildness, moreover, is drawing toward total darkness,
and inclining toward the silent blue. Meanwhile, the poet him-

self, on "black cloud," travels over "the nighting pond, the starry sky."

The poem goes:

Ghostly Twilight

Still at the forest's edge meets
Dark wild game;
On the hill, evening breeze softly expires,

Blackbird's plaint falls silent,
And the gentle flutes of autumn
Hush in the rushes.

On black cloud, you
Drunk with poppy travel
The nighting pond,

The starry sky.
Always the sister's lunar voice
Sounds through the ghostly night.

The starry sky is portrayed in the poetic image of the nighting pond. Such would be our usual notion. But the night sky, in the truth of its nature, is this pond. By contrast, what we otherwise call night remains rather a mere image, the pale and empty counterfeit of night's nature. The pond and the pond's mirror recur often in the poet's work. The waters, which are sometimes black and sometimes blue, show to man his own countenance, his countering glance. But in the nighting pond of the starry sky there appears the twilight blue of the ghostly night. Its glance is cool.

The cool light issues from the shining of Dame Moon (*selanna*). All around her radiance, as the ancient Greek verses tell us, the stars turn pale and even cool. All things become "lunar." The stranger going through the night is called "the lunar one" (128). The sister's lunar voice forever ringing through the night is heard by the brother who, in his boat that is still "black" and barely illumined by the stranger's golden radiance, tries to follow the stranger's nocturnal course upon the pond.

When mortals follow after the "something strange," that is

to say, after the stranger who is called to go under, they themselves enter strangeness, they themselves become strangers and solitary.

Only through its course on the night's starry pond—which is the sky above the earth—does the soul experience the earth in its "cool sap" (120). The soul slips away into the evening blue of the ghostly year. It becomes the "autumnal soul" and as such the "blue soul."

The few stanzas and lines noted here point into the ghostly twilight, lead onto the stranger's path, and indicate the kind and the course of those who, recalling him, follow him to go under. At the time of "Summer's Decline," the strangeness in his wandering becomes autumnal and dark.

One of Trakl's poems which he entitled "Autumnal Soul" sings in the second stanza from the end (118) :

> Fish and game soon glide away.
> Soon blue soul and long dark journey
> Parted us from loved ones, others.
> Evening changes image, sense.

The wanderers who follow the stranger soon find themselves parted "from loved ones" who to them are "others." The others —that is the cast of the decomposed form of man.

A human cast, cast in one mold and cast away into this cast, is called a kin, of a kind, a generation. The word refers to mankind as a whole as well as to kinship in the sense of race, tribe, family—all of these in turn cast in the duality of the sexes. The cast of man's "decomposed form" is what the poet calls the "decomposing" kind (129). It is the generation that has been removed from its kind of essential being, and this is why it is the "unsettled" kind (156).

What curse has struck this humankind? The curse of the decomposing kind is that the old human kinship has been struck apart by discord among sexes, tribes and races. Each strives to escape from that discord into the unleashed turmoil of the always isolated and sheer wildness of the wild game. Not duality as such, the discord is the curse. Out of the turmoil of blind wildness it carries each kind into an irreconcilable split, and so casts it into unbridled isolation. The "fragmented kind," so cleft in two, can on its own no longer find its proper cast. Its proper cast is only with that kind whose duality leaves discord behind and leads the way, as "something strange," into the gentleness of simple twofoldness following in the stranger's footsteps.

With respect to that stranger, all the progeny of the decomposing kind remain the others. Even so, love and reverence are attached to them. But the dark journey in the stranger's train brings them into the blue of his night. The wandering soul becomes the "blue soul."

But at the same time the soul is also set apart. Where to? To where the stranger walks, who at times is poetically called only "he yonder." "He yonder," the stranger, is the other one to the others, to the decomposing kind. He is the one who has been called away from others. The stranger is he who is apart.

Whither is such a being directed which itself assumes the nature of the strange, that it must wander ahead? In what direction is a strange thing called? It is called to go under—to lose itself in the ghostly twilight of the blue, to incline with the decline toward the ghostly year. While this decline must pass through the destructiveness of approaching winter, through November, to lose itself yet does not mean that it crumbles into a shambles and is annihilated. On the contrary, to lose oneself means literally to loosen one's bonds and slowly slip away. He who loses himself does of course disappear in the November destruction, but he does not slip into it. He slips through it, away into the blue's ghostly twilight "at vespers," toward evening.

> At vespers the stranger loses himself in
>   black November destruction,
> Under rotting branches, along the leprous walls,
> Where the holy brother had gone before,
> Lost in the soft lyre music of his madness.

>   (*Helian*, 81)

Evening is the decline of the days of the ghostly year.
Evening consummates a change. Evening which inclines to the
ghostly gives us other things to contemplate and to ponder.

The luminous appearances of whose aspects (images) the
poets have their say appear differently in the light of this
evening. The essential reality that thinkers try to grasp in
thought speaks other words with the onset of this evening.
From another sense and another image, evening transmutes
all saying of poetry and thinking, and their dialogue. But
evening can do so only because it, too, changes. Day goes
through evening into a decline that is not an end, but simply
an inclination to make ready that descent by which the
stranger goes under into the *beginning* of his wandering.
Evening changes its own image and its own sense. This change
conceals a departure from the traditional order of days and
seasons.

But whither does evening accompany the blue soul's dark
wandering? To the place where everything has come together
in another way, where everything is sheltered and preserved
for an other ascent.

The stanzas and lines quoted so far bring us to a gathering,
that is to say, they bring us to a site. Of what kind is this
site? What shall we name it? Surely the name must fit the
poet's language. All that Georg Trakl's poetry says remains
gathered and focused on the wandering stranger. He is, and
is called, "he who is apart" (170). Through him and around
him Trakl's poetic saying is tuned to one unique song. And
since this poet's poems are gathered into the song of him who
is apart, we shall call the site of Trakl's poetic work *apartness*.

And now, by a second step, our discussion must try to gain a
clearer view of this site which so far has only been pointed out.

II

Is it possible to bring apartness itself before our mind's
eye, to contemplate it as the poem's site? If at all, it can be
done only if we now follow the stranger's path with clearer
eyes, and ask: Who is the departed one? What is the landscape of his paths?

His paths run through the blue of night. The light that gives his steps their radiance is cool. The closing words of a poem devoted specifically to the "departed one" speak of "the lunar paths of the departed" (171). To us, departed also means deceased. But into what kind of death has the stranger died? In his poem "Psalm" (57), Trakl says:

> The madman has died

The next stanza says:

> They bury the stranger.

In the "Seven-Song of Death" he is called the "white stranger." The last stanza of "Psalm" ends with this line:

> In his grave the white magician plays with his snakes.

The dead one *lives* in his grave. He lives in his chamber, so quietly and lost in thought that he plays with his snakes. They cannot harm him. They have not been strangled, but their malice has been transformed. In the poem "The Accursed" (113), on the other hand, we find:

> A nest of scarlet-colored snakes rears up
> Lazily in her churned-up lap.
>
> (Compare 155 and 157)

The dead one is the madman. Does the word mean someone who is mentally ill? Madness here does not mean a mind filled with senseless delusions. The madman's mind senses—senses in fact as no one else does. Even so, he does not have the sense of the others. He is of another mind. The departed one is a man apart, a madman, because he has taken his way in another direction. From that other direction, his madness may be called "gentle," for his mind pursues a greater stillness. A poem that refers to the stranger simply as "he yonder," the other one, sings:

> But the other descended the stone steps of the
> Mönchsberg,
> A blue smile on his face and strangely ensheathed
> In his quieter childhood and died.

This poem is called "To One who Died Young" (129). The

departed died away early. That is why he is "the tender corpse" (99, 139, etc.), shrouded in that childhood which preserves in greater stillness all the burning and searing of the wilderness. He who died early thus appears as the "dark shape of coolness." This shape also appears in the poem entitled "On the Mönchsberg" (107):

> The dark shape of coolness ever follows the
> wanderer
> Over the footbridge of bone, and the boy's hyacinth
> voice,
> Softly reciting the forest's forgotten legend . . .

The "dark shape of coolness" does not follow behind the wanderer. It walks before him, because the boy's blue voice retrieves something forgotten and *fore-tells* it.

Who is this boy that died away early? Who is this boy to whom it is said

> . . . softly your forehead bleeds
> Ancient legends
> And dark augury of the flight of birds? (91)

Who is he who has crossed over the bridge of bone? The poet calls to him with the words:

> O Elis, how long you have been dead.

Elis is the stranger called to go under. He is in no way a figure by which Trakl means to represent himself. Elis is as essentially different from the poet Trakl as Zarathustra's figure is from the thinker Nietzsche. But both figures are alike in that their nature and their journey begins with a descent. Elis goes down into the primeval earliness that is older than the aged, decomposing kind of man, older because it is more mindful, more mindful because it is more still, more still because it has itself a greater power to still.

The boyishness in the figure of the boy Elis does not consist in the opposite of girlishness. His boyishness is the appearance of his stiller childhood. That childhood shelters and stores within it the gentle two-fold of sex, the youth and the "golden figure of the maiden" (172).

Elis is not a dead who decays and ceases to be in the lateness of a spent life. Elis is the dead whose being moves away
into earliness. This stranger unfolds human nature forward
into the beginning of what is yet to be borne. This unborn
element in the nature of mortals, which is quieter and hence
more stilling, is what the poet calls the unborn.

The stranger who has died away into earliness is the unborn
one. The terms "something unborn" and "something strange"
say the same. In the poem "Bright Spring" (21) there is this
line:

> And the unborn tends to its own peace.

It guards and watches over the stiller childhood for the coming
awakening of mankind. Thus at rest, the early dead *lives*. The
departed one is not dead in the sense of being spent. On the
contrary. The departed looks forward into the blue of the
ghostly night. The white eyelids that protect his vision gleam
with the bridal adornment (133) that promises the gentler
two-fold of humankind.

> Silent the myrtle blooms over his dead white eyelids.

This line belongs in the same poem that says:

> Something strange is the soul on the earth.

The two sentences stand close to each other. The "dead" is the
departed, the stranger, the unborn.

But still the "path of the unborn" leads "past gloomy towns,
past lonely summers" ("Song of the Hours," 95). His way leads
past those things that will not receive him as a guest, past but
already no longer through them. The departed one's journey
is lonely, too, of course—but that comes from the loneliness
of "the nighting pond, the starry sky." The madman crosses
the pond not on a "black cloud" but in a golden boat. What
about the gold? The poem "Corner by the Forest" (29) replies
with the line:

> Gentle madness also often sees the golden, the true.

The stranger's path leads through the "ghostly years" whose days are everywhere turned toward the beginning and are ruled, set right, from there. The year of his soul is gathered into rightness.

> O how righteous, Elis, are all your days

sings the poem "Elis" (92). This call is merely the echo of the other call, heard before:

> O Elis, how long you have been dead.

The earliness into which the stranger has expired shelters the essential rightness of the unborn. This earliness is a time of its own kind, the time of the "ghostly years." To one of his poems, Trakl gave the plain title "Year" (164). It begins: "Dark stillness of childhood." The counterpart to that dark stillness is the brighter earliness—brighter because it is an even stiller and therefore other childhood—into which the departed has gone under. The last line of the same poem calls this stiller childhood the beginning:

> Golden eye of the beginning, dark patience of the end.

Here, the end is not the sequel and fading echo of the beginning. The end—being the end of the decaying kind—precedes the beginning of the unborn kind. But the beginning, the earlier earliness, has already overtaken the end.

That earliness preserves the original nature—a nature so far still veiled—of time. This nature will go on being impenetrable to the dominant mode of thinking as long as the Aristotelian concept of time, still standard everywhere, retains its currency. According to this concept, time—whether conceived mechanically or dynamically or in terms of atomic decay—is the dimension of the quantitative or qualitative calculation of duration as a sequential progression.

True time, however, is the arrival of that which has been. This is not what is past, but rather the gathering of essential being, which precedes all arrival in gathering itself into the shelter of what it was earlier, before the given moment. The end and accomplishment has its analogue in "dark patience." Patience bears hidden things toward their truth. Its forbearance bears everything toward its descent down into the blue of the ghostly night. The beginning, on the other hand, corresponds to a seeing and minding which gleams golden because it is illuminated by "the golden, the true." This gold and true is reflected in the starry pond of night when Elis on his journey opens his heart to the night (92) :

> A golden boat
> Sways, Elis, your heart against a lonely sky.

The stranger's boat tosses, playful rather than "timorously" (192) , like the boat of those descendants of earliness who still merely follow the stranger. Their boat does not yet reach the level of the pond's surface. It sinks. But where? Does it go under in decay? No. And into what does it sink? Into empty nothingness? Far from it. One of Trakl's last poems, "Lament" (192) , ends with the lines:

> Sister of stormy sadness,
> Look, a timorous boat goes down
> Under stars,
> The silent face of the night.

What does this nocturnal silence hold that looks down out of the starlight? Where does this silence itself with its night belong? To apartness. This apartness is more than merely the state in which the boy Elis lives, the state of being dead.

The earliness of stiller childhood, the blue night, the stranger's nighting paths, the soul's nocturnal wing-beat, even the twilight as the gateway to descent: all these belong to apartness.

All these are gathered up into apartness, not afterward but such that apartness unfolds within their already established gathering.

Twilight, night, the stranger's years, his paths, all are called "ghostly" by the poet. The apartness is "ghostly." This word— what does it mean? Its meaning and its use are very old.

"Ghostly" means what is by way of the spirit, stems from it
and follows its nature. "Ghostly" means spiritual, but not in
the narrow sense that ties the word to "spirituality," the priestly
orders or their church. To a superficial reader, even Trakl
seems to use the word in this narrow sense, at least in the poem
"In Hellbrunn" (183), where it says:

> . . . Thus the oaks turn spiritually green,
> Above the dead's forgotten paths.

Earlier, the poet mentions "the shades of princes of the church,
of noble women," "the shades of those long dead" which seem
to hover above the "pond of spring." But the poet, who is here
again singing "the blue lament of evening," does not think of
the clergy when he says "the oaks turn spiritually green." He
is thinking of that earliness of the long since dead which
promises the "springtime of the soul." The poem "Song of the
Spirit" (16), composed earlier, strikes the same theme, though
in an even more veiled and searching manner. The spirit
referred to in this strangely ambiguous "Song of the Spirit"
finds clearer expression in the last stanza:

> Beggar there by ancient stone
> Seems expired in a prayer,
> Shepherd gently leaves the hill,
> In the grove an angel sings,
> Sings a song,
> Sings the children to their sleep.

But, even though the word "spiritual" has no ecclesiastical
overtones for the poet himself, he surely could have resorted
to the phrase "of the spirit" to refer to what he has in mind,
and speak of twilight of the spirit and night of the spirit. Why
does he not do so? Because "of the spirit" means the opposite
of material. This opposition posits a differentiation of two
separate realms and, in Platonic-Western terms, states the gulf
between the suprasensuous *noeton* and the sensuous *aistheton*.

"Of the spirit" so understood—it meanwhile has come to mean rational, intellectual, ideological—together with its opposites belongs to the world view of the decaying kind of man. But the "dark journey" of the "blue soul" parts company with this kind. The twilight leading toward the night in which the strangeness goes under deserves as little to be called "of the spirit, intellectual" as does the stranger's path. Apartness is spiritual, determined by the spirit, and ghostly, but it is not "of the spirit" in the sense of the language of metaphysics.

What, then, is the spirit? In his last poem, "Grodek" (193), Trakl speaks of the "hot flame of the spirit." The spirit is flaming, and only in this sense perhaps is it something flickering in the air. Trakl sees spirit not primarily as *pneuma*, something ethereal, but as a flame that inflames, startles, horrifies, and shatters us. Flame is glowing lumination. What flame is the *ek-stasis* which lightens and calls forth radiance, but which may also go on consuming and reduce all to white ashes.

"Flame is the palest pallor's brother" runs a line in the poem "Transformation of Evil" (123). Trakl sees spirit in terms of that being which is indicated in the original meaning of the word "ghost"—a being terrified, beside himself, *ek-static*.

Spirit or ghost understood in this way has its being in the possibility of *both* gentleness *and* destructiveness. Gentleness in no way dampens the ecstasy of the inflammatory, but holds it gathered in the peace of friendship. Destructiveness comes from unbridled license, which consumes itself in its own revolt and thus is active evil. Evil is always the evil of a ghostly spirit. Evil and its malice is not of a sensuous, material nature. Nor is it purely "of the spirit." Evil is ghostly in that it is the revolt of a terror blazing away in blind delusion, which casts all things into unholy fragmentation and threatens to turn the calm, collected blossoming of gentleness to ashes.

But where does the gathering power of gentleness reside? How is it bridled? What spirit holds its reins? In what way is human nature ghostly, and how does it become so?

Inasmuch as the nature of spirit consists in a bursting into flame, it strikes a new course, lights it, and sets man on the way. Being flame, the spirit is the storm that "storms the heavens" and "hunts down God" (180). The spirit chases, drives the soul to get underway to where it leads the way. The spirit carries it over into strangeness. "Something strange is the soul on the earth." The soul is the gift of the spirit—the spirit animates. But the soul in turn guards the spirit, so essentially that without the soul the spirit can presumably never be spirit. The soul "feeds" the spirit. How? How else than by investing the spirit with the flame that is in the soul's very nature? This flame is the glow of melancholy, "the patience of the lonely soul" (51).

Solitude does not separate in the kind of dispersion to which all mere forsakenness is exposed. Solitude carries the soul toward the One and only, gathers it into the One, and so starts its being out on its journey. Solitary, the soul is a wanderer. The ardor of its core is charged to carry on its journey the burden of fate—and so to carry the soul toward the spirit.

> Lend your flame to the spirit, ardent and heavy heart;

so begins the poem "To Lucifer," in other words, the poem to the light-bearer who casts the shadow of evil (posthumous volume, Salzburg edition, p. 14).

The soul's heavy heart glows only when the wandering soul enters into the farthest reaches of its essential being—its wandering nature. That happens when the soul looks toward the face of the blue and beholds its radiance. In that seeing it is "the great soul."

> O pain, thou flaming vision
> Of the great soul!
>
> (*Thunderstorm*, 175)

The soul's greatness takes its measure from its capacity to achieve the flaming vision by which the soul becomes at home in pain. The nature of pain is in itself converse.

"Flaming" pain tears away. Pain's rending, sweeping force consigns the wandering soul into that conjunction of storm and hunt which would storm heaven and hunt down God.

Thus it seems as though the stormy sweep were to overwhelm its goal, instead of letting it prevail within its veiling radiance.

Yet this latter is within the power of the beholding "vision." That vision does not quench the flaming sweep, but rejoins it to the fitting submission of seeing acceptance. It is that backward sweep in pain by which pain achieves its mildness, its power to disclose and convey.

Spirit is flame. It glows and shines. Its shining takes place in the beholding look. To such a vision is given the advent of all that shines, where all that is, is present. This flaming vision is pain. Its nature remains impenetrable to any mind that understands pain in terms of sensitivity. Flaming vision determines the soul's greatness.

The spirit which bears the gift of the "great soul" is pain; pain is the animator. And the soul so gifted is the giver of life. This is why everything that is alive in the sense in which the soul is alive, is imbued with pain, the fundamental trait of the soul's nature. Everything that is alive, is painful.

Only a being that lives soulfully can fulfill the destiny of its nature. By virtue of this power it is fit to join in that harmony of mutual bearing by which all living things belong together. In keeping with this relation of fitness, everything that lives is fit, that is to say, good. But the good is good painfully.

Corresponding to the great soul's fundamental trait, everything that has soul is not merely good painfully, but also it can be truthful only in that way; for, in virtue of the fact that pain is converse, the living can give sheltering concealment to their present fellowbeings and thus reveal them in their given nature, let them truly be what they are.

The last stanza of one poem begins (22) :

> So painful good, so truthful is what lives;

One might think that this line merely touches on what is painful. In truth it introduces the saying of the entire stanza, which remains tuned to the silent conquest of pain. To hear it, we must not overlook the carefully placed punctuation, much less alter it. The stanza goes on:

> And softly touches you an ancient stone:

Again this "softly" is sounded, which always leads us softly to the essential relations. Again the "stone" appears which, if calculation were permitted here, could be counted in more than thirty places in Trakl's poetry. Pain conceals itself in the stone, the petrifying pain that delivers itself into the keeping of the impenetrable rock in whose appearance there shines forth its ancient origin out of the silent glow of the first dawn— the earliest dawn which, as the prior beginning, is coming toward everything that is becoming, and brings to it the advent, never to be overtaken, of its essential being.

The old stones are pain itself, for pain looks earthily upon mortals. The colon after the word "stone" signifies that now *the stone* is speaking. Pain itself has the word. Silent since long ago, it now says to the wanderers who follow the stranger nothing less than its own power and endurance:

> Truly! I shall forever be with you.

The wanderers who listen toward the leafy branches for the early dead, reply to these words of pain with the words of the next line:

> O mouth! that trembles through the silvery willow.

The whole stanza here corresponds to the close of another poem's second stanza, addressed "To One Who Died Young" (129):

> And the silver face of his friend stayed behind in the garden,
> Listening in the leaves or the ancient stones.

The stanza which begins

> So painful good, so truthful is what lives;

also resolves the chord struck in the first line of the same poem's third section:

> How sick seems all that is becoming!

The troubled, hampered, dismal, and diseased, all the distress of disintegrating, is in truth nothing else than the single semblance in which truth—truly—conceals itself: the all-pervading, everlasting pain. Pain is thus neither repugnant nor profitable. Pain is the benignity in the nature of all essential being. The onefold simplicity of its converse nature determines all becoming out of concealed primal earliness, and attunes it to the bright serenity of the great soul.

> So painful good, so truthful is what lives,
> And softly touches you an ancient stone:
> Truly! I shall forever be with you.
> O mouth! that trembles through the silvery willow.

The stanza is the pure song of pain, sung to complete the three-part poem called "Bright Spring" (21). The primal early brightness of all dawning being trembles out of the stillness of concealed pain.

To our customary way of thinking, the converse nature of pain—that its sweep carries us truly onward only as it sweeps us back—may easily seem self-contradictory. But beneath this semblance is concealed the essential onefold simplicity of pain. Flaming, it carries farthest when it holds to itself most intimately in contemplating vision.

Thus pain, the great soul's fundamental trait, remains pure harmony with the holiness of the blue. For the blue shines upon the soul's face by withdrawing into its own depth. Whenever it is present, the holy endures only by keeping within this withdrawal, and by turning vision toward the fitting.

The nature of pain, its concealed relation to the blue, is put into words in the last stanza of a poem called "Transfiguration" (137):

> Blue flower,
> That softly sounds in withered stone.

The "blue flower" is the "gentle cornflower sheaf" of the ghostly night. The words sing of the wellspring from which

Trakl's poetry wells up. They conclude, and also carry, the "tranfiguration." The song is lyric, tragedy, and epic all in one. This poem is unique among them all, because in it the breadth of vision, the depth of thought, and the simplicity of saying shine intimate and everlasting, ineffably.

Pain is truly pain only when it serves the flame of the spirit. Trakl's last poem is called "Grodek." It has been much praised as a war poem. But it is infinitely more, because it is something other. Its final lines (193) are:

> Today a great pain feeds the hot flame of the spirit,
> The grandsons yet unborn.

These "grandsons" are not the unbegotten sons of the sons killed in battle, the progeny of the decaying generation. If that were all, merely an end to the procreation of earlier generations, our poet would have to rejoice over such an end. But he grieves, though with a "prouder grief" that flamingly contemplates the peace of the unborn.

The unborn are called grandsons because they cannot be sons, that is, they cannot be the immediate descendants of the generation that has gone to ruin. Another generation lives between these two. It is other, for it is of another kind in keeping with its different essential origin in the earliness of what is still unborn. The "mighty pain" is the beholding vision whose flames envelop everything, and which looks ahead into the still-withdrawing earliness of yonder dead one toward whom the "ghosts" of early victims have died.

But who guards this mighty pain, that it may feed the hot flame of the spirit? Whatever is akin to this spirit is of the kind that starts man on the way. Whatever is akin to this spirit is called "ghostly." And thus the poet must call "ghostly" the twilight, the night, and the years—these above all and these alone. The twilight makes the blue of night to rise, inflames it. Night flames as the shining mirror of the starry pond. The year inflames by starting the sun's course on its way, its risings and its settings.

What spirit is it from which this "ghostliness" awakens and

which it follows? It is the spirit which in the poem "To One Who Died Young" (129) is specifically called "the spirit of an early dead." It is the spirit which abandons that "beggar" of the "Spiritual Song" (16) to his apartness, so that he, as the poem "In the Village" (75) says, remains "the poor one," "who died lonesome in spirit."

Apartness is active as pure spirit. It is the radiance of the blue reposing in the spirit's depth and flaming in greater stillness, the blue that kindles a stiller childhood into the gold of the first beginning. This is the earliness toward which Elis' golden countenance is turned. In its countering glance, it keeps alive the nocturnal flame of the spirit of apartness.

Apartness, then, is neither merely the state of him who died young, nor the indeterminate realm of his abode. In the way in which it flames, apartness itself is the spirit and thus the gathering power. That power carries mortal nature back to its stiller childhood, and shelters that childhood as the kind, not yet borne to term, whose stamp marks future generations. The gathering power of apartness holds the unborn generation beyond all that is spent, and saves it for a coming rebirth of mankind out of earliness. The gathering power, spirit of gentleness, stills also the spirit of evil. That spirit's revolt rises to its utmost malice when it breaks out even from the discord of the sexes, and invades the realm of brother and sister.

But in the stiller onefold simplicity of childhood is hidden also the kindred twofoldness of mankind. In apartness, the spirit of evil is neither destroyed and denied, nor set free and affirmed. Evil is transformed. To endure such a "transformation," the soul must turn to the greatness of its nature. The spirit of apartness determines how great this greatness is. Apartness is the gathering through which human nature is sheltered once again in its stiller childhood, and that childhood in turn is sheltered in the earliness of another beginning. As a gathering, apartness is in the nature of a site.

But in what way, now, is apartness the site of a poetic work, specifically that poetic statement to which Trakl's poetry gives voice? Is apartness at all and intrinsically related to poetry? Even if such a relation exists, how is apartness to gather poetic saying to itself, to become its site, and to determine it from there?

Is apartness not one single silence of stillness? How can it start a saying and a singing on its way? Yet apartness is not the desolation of the departed dead. In apartness, the stranger measures off the parting from mankind hitherto. He is underway on a path. What sort of a path is it? The poet says it plainly enough, by pointedly setting apart the closing line of the poem "Summer's Decline";

> Would that the blue game were to recall his paths,
>
> The music of his ghostly years!

The stranger's path is the "music of his ghostly years." Elis' footfall rings. The ringing footfall radiates through the night. Does its music die away into a void? He who died into earliness—is he departed in the sense of being cut off, or has he been set apart because he is one of the select—gathered up into an assembly· that gathers more gently and calls more quietly?

The second and third stanzas of the poem "To One Who Died Young" (129) hint at an answer:

> But he yonder descended the stone steps of the Mönchsberg,
> A blue smile on his face, and strangely ensheathed
> In his stiller childhood, and died;
> And the silver face of his friend stayed behind in the garden,
> Listening in the leaves or the ancient stones.
>
> Soul sang of death, the green decay of the flesh,
> And it was the murmur of the forest,
> The fervid lament of the animals.
> Always from twilight towers rang the blue evening bells.

A friend listens after the stranger. In listening, he follows the departed and thus becomes himself a wanderer, a stranger. The friend's soul listens after the dead. The friend's face has "died away" (136). It listens by singing of death. This is why the singing voice is "the birdvoice of the deathlike" (*The Wanderer,* 136). It corresponds to the stranger's death, his going under to the blue of night. But as he sings the death of the departed, he also sings the "green decay" of that generation from which his dark journey has "parted" him.

To sing means to praise and to guard the object of praise in song. The listening friend is one of the "praising shepherds" (136). Yet the friend's soul, which "likes to listen to the white magician's fairy tales," can give echo to the song of the departed only when that apartness rings out toward him who follows, when the music of apartness resounds, "when," as it says in "Evensong" (77), "dark music haunts the soul."

If all this comes to pass, the spirit of the early dead appears in the glow of earliness. The ghostly years of earliness are the true time of the stranger and his friend. In their glow the formerly black cloud turns golden. Now it is like that "golden boat" which, Elis' heart, rocks in the solitary sky.

The last stanza of "To One Who Died Young" (130) sings;

> Golden cloud and time. In a lonely room
> You often ask the dead to visit you,
> And walk in trusted converse under elms by the
>   green stream.

The friend's invitation to conversation reflects the haunting music of the stranger's steps. The friend's saying is the singing journey down by the stream, following down into the blue of the night that is animated by the spirit of the early dead. In such conversation the singing friend gazes upon the departed. By his gaze, in the converse look, he becomes brother to the stranger. Journeying with the stranger, the brother reaches the stiller abode in earliness. In the "Song of the Departed" (170), he can call out:

> O to dwell in the animate blue of night.

Listening after the departed, the friend sings his song and

thus becomes his brother; only now, as the stranger's brother, does he also become the brother of the stranger's sister whose "lunar voice rings through the ghostly night," as the last lines of "Ghostly Twilight" (131) say it.

Apartness is the poem's site because the music of the stranger's ringing-radiant footfall inflames his followers' dark wandering into listening song. The dark wandering, dark because it merely follows after, nevertheless clears their souls toward the blue. Then the whole being of the singing soul is one single concentrated gaze ahead into the blue of night which holds that stiller earliness.

Soul then is purely a blue moment

is what the poem "Childhood" (98) says about it.

Thus the nature of apartness is perfected. It is the perfect site of the poetic work only when, being both the gathering of the stiller childhood and the stranger's grave, it gathers to itself also those who follow him who died early, by listening after him and carrying the music of his path over into the sounds of spoken language, so that they become men apart. Their song is poetry. How so? What is the poet's work?

The poet's work means: to say after—to say again the music of the spirit of apartness that has been spoken to the poet. For the longest time—before it comes to be said, that is, spoken—the poet's work is only a listening. Apartness first gathers the listening into its music, so that this music may ring through the spoken saying in which it will resound. The lunar coolness of the ghostly night's holy blue rings and shines through all such gazing and saying. Its language becomes a saying-after, it becomes: poetry. Poetry's spoken words shelter the poetic statement as that which by its essential nature remains unspoken. In this manner, the saying-after, thus called upon to listen, becomes "more pious," that is to say, more pliable to the promptings of the path on which the stranger walks ahead, out of the dark of childhood into the stiller, brighter earliness. The poet listening after him can thus say to himself:

More pious now, you know the dark years' meaning,
Autumn and cool in solitary rooms;
And in holier blue radiant footfalls ring.

(*Childhood*, 98)

The soul that sings of autumn and the year's decline is not sinking in decay. Its piety is kindled by the flame of the spirit of earliness, and therefore is fiery:

O the soul that softly sang the song of the
withered reeds; flaming piety.

says the poem "Dream and Shroud of Night" (151). This shroud of night is not a mere darkening of the mind, no more than madness is dementedness. The night that shrouds the stranger's singing brother remains the "ghostly night" of that death by which the departed died into the "golden tremor" of earliness. Gazing after him, the listening friend looks out into the coolness of childhood's greater stillness. But such gazing remains a parting from that cast of man, long since born, which has forgot the stiller childhood as the beginning that is still in store, and has never carried the unborn to full term. The poem "Anif" (128), named after a moated castle near Salzburg, says:

Great is the guilt of the born. Woe, you golden tremor
Of death,
When the soul dreams cooler blossoms.

But that "woe" of pain embraces not only the parting *from* the old kinship. This parting is in a hidden and fated way set apart, set to take the departure called for by apartness. The wandering in the night of apartness is "infinite torment." This does not mean unending agony. The infinite is devoid of all finite restriction and stuntedness. The "infinite torment" is consummate, perfect pain, pain that comes to the fullness of its nature. The simple oneness of pain's converse character comes into pure play only during the journey through the ghostly night, a journey that always takes its parting from the unghostly night. The spirit's gentle-

ness is called to hunt down God, its shy reserve called to
storm heaven.

In the poem "The Night" (180), it says:

> Infinite torment,
> That you hunted down God
> Gentle spirit,
> Sighing in the cataract,
> In the waving fir trees.

The flaming rapture of this storm and hunt does not tear
"the steep-walled fortress" down; it does not lay the quarry
low, but lets it arise to behold the sights of heaven whose
pure coolness veils the Divine. The singing reflection of such
wandering belongs to the brow of a head marked by consummate pain. The poem "The Night" therefore closes with
the lines:

> A petrified head
> Storms heaven.

Correspondingly, the end of the poem "The Heart" (172) runs:

> The steep-walled fortress.
> O heart
> Shimmering away into snowy coolness.

In fact, the triadic harmony of the three late poems "The
Heart," "The Storm," and "The Night" is so subtly tuned
to One and the Same singing of apartness that the discussion
of the poetic work here attempted is further prompted
simply to leave those three poems to resound in their song
without intruding an elucidation.

Wandering in apartness, beholding the sights of the invisible, and consummate pain—they belong together. The
patient one submits to pain's sweep. He alone is able to
follow the return into the primal earliness of the generation
whose fate is preserved in an old album in which the poet
inscribes the following stanza called "In an Old Album" (51):

> Humbly the patient one bows to the pain
> Ringing with music and with soft madness.
> Look! the twilight appears.

In such soft and sweet-sounding saying the poet brings to radiance the luminous sights in which God conceals himself from the mad hunt. It is thus only "Whispered into the Afternoon" when, in a poem (50) by that title, the poet sings:

> God's own colors dreams my brow,
> Feels the gentle wings of madness.

The poet becomes poet only as he follows that "madman" who died away into the early dawn and who now from his apartness, by the music of his footfall, calls to the brother who follows him. Thus the friend's face looks into the face of the stranger. The radiance of the glancing moment moves the listener's saying. In the moving radiance that shines from the site of the poem surges the billow which starts the poetic vision on its way to language.

Of what sort, then, is the language of Trakl's poetic work? It speaks by answering to that journey upon which the stranger is leading on ahead. The path he has taken leads away from the old degenerate generation. It escorts him to go under in the carliness of the unborn generation that is kept in store. The language of the poetry whose site is in apartness answers to the home-coming of unborn mankind into the quiet beginning of its stiller nature.

The language that this poetry speaks stems from this transition. Its path leads from the downfall of all that decays over to the descent into the twilit blue of the holy. The language that the work speaks stems from the passage across and through the ghostly night's nocturnal pond. This language sings the song of the home-coming in apartness, the home-coming which from the lateness of decomposition comes to rest in the earliness of the stiller, and still impending, beginning. In this language there speaks the journey whose shining causes the radiant, ringing music of the departed stranger's ghostly years to come forth. According to the words of the poem "Revelation and Descent" (186), the "Song of the Departed" sings of "the beauty of a homecoming generation."

Because the language of this poetry speaks from the journey

of apartness, it will always speak also of what it leaves behind in parting, and of that to which the departure submits. This language is essentially ambiguous, in its own fashion. We shall hear nothing of what the poem says so long as we bring to it only this or that dull sense of unambiguous meaning.

Twilight and night, descent and death, madness and wild game, pond and stone, bird's flight and boat, stranger and brother, ghost and God, and also the words of color—blue and green, white and black, red and silver, gold and dark—all say ever and again manifold things.

"Green" is decay *and* bloom, "white" pale *and* pure, "black" is enclosing in gloom *and* darkly sheltering, "red" fleshy purple *and* gentle rose. "Silver" is the pallor of death and the sparkle of the stars. "Gold" is the glow of truth as well as "grisly laughter of gold" (127). These examples of multiple meanings are so far only two-sided. But their ambiguousness, taken as a whole, becomes but one side of a greater issue, whose other side is determined by the poetry's innermost site.

The poetic work speaks out of an ambiguous ambiguousness. Yet this multiple ambiguousness of the poetic saying does not scatter in vague equivocations. The ambiguous tone of Trakl's poetry arises out of a gathering, that is, out of a unison which, meant for itself alone, always remains unsayable. The ambiguity of this poetic saying is not lax imprecision, but rather the rigor of him who leaves what is as it is, who has entered into the "righteous vision" and now submits to it.

It is often hard for us to draw a clear line between the ambiguous saying characteristic of Trakl's poems—which in his work shows complete assurance—and the language of other poets whose equivocations stem from the vagueness of groping poetic uncertainty, because their language lacks authentic poetry and its site. The peerless rigor of Trakl's essentially ambiguous language is in a higher sense so unequivocal that it remains infinitely superior even to all the technical precision of concepts that are merely scientifically univocal.

This same ambiguity of language that is determined by the site of Trakl's poetic work also inspires his frequent use of

words from the world of biblical and ecclesiastical ideas. The
passage from the old to the unborn generation leads through
this region and its language. Whether Trakl's poems speak in
a Christian fashion, to what extent and in what sense, in what
way Trakl was a "Christian," what is meant here, and indeed
generally, by "Christian," "Christianity," "Christendom" and
"Christlike": all this involves essential questions. But their discussion hangs in a void so long as the site of his poetic work is
not thoughtfully established. Besides, their discussion calls for
a kind of thorough thinking to which neither the concept of a
metaphysical nor those of a church-based theology are adequate.

To judge the Christianity of Trakl's poetic work, one would
have to give thought above all to his last two poems, "Lament"
and "Grodek." One would have to ask: If indeed this poet is
so resolute a Christian, why does he not, here in the extreme
agony of his last saying, call out to God and Christ? Why does
he instead name the "sister's swaying shadow" and call her
"the greeting one"? Why does the song end with the name of
the "unborn grandsons" and not with the confident hope of
Christian redemption? Why does the sister appear also in the
other late poem, "Lament" (192) ? Why is eternity called there
"the icy wave"? Is this Christian thinking? It is not even
Christian despair.

But what does this "Lament" sing of? In these words, "Sister
. . . Look . . . ," does not an intimate ardent simplicity ring
out, the simplicity of those who remain on the journey toward
the "golden face of man," despite the danger of the utter withdrawal of all wholeness?

The rigorous unison of the many-voiced language in which
Trakl's poetry speaks—and this means also: is silent—corresponds to apartness as the site of his work. Merely to keep this
site rightly in mind makes demands on our thinking. We
hardly dare in closing to ask for the location of this site.

III

When we took the first step in our discussion of Trakl's poetic
work, the poem "Autumn Soul" (118), in its second-to-last

stanza, gave us the final indication that apartness is the site of his poetry. That stanza speaks of those wanderers who follow the stranger's path through the ghostly night in order that they may "dwell in its animate blue."

> Fish and game soon glide away.
> Soon blue soul and long dark journey
> Parted us from loved ones, others.

An open region that holds the promise of a dwelling, and provides a dwelling, is what we call a "land." The passage into the stranger's land leads through ghostly twilight, in the evening. This is why the last stanze runs:

> Evening changes image, sense.

The land into which the early dead goes down is the land of this evening. The location of the site that gathers Trakl's work into itself is the concealed nature of apartness, and is called "Evening Land," the Occident. This land is older, which is to say, earlier and therefore more promising than the Platonic-Christian land, or indeed than a land conceived in terms of the European West. For apartness is the "first beginning" of a mounting world-year, not the abyss of decay.

The evening land concealed in apartness is not going down; it stays and, as the land of descent into the ghostly night, awaits those who will dwell in it. The land of descent is the transition into the beginning of the dawn concealed within it.

If we keep these thoughts in mind, we surely cannot then dismiss as mere coincidence the fact that two of Trakl's poems speak explicitly of the land of evening. One bears the title "Evening Land" or "Occident" (165) the other is called "Occidental Song" (133): it sings the same as does the "Song of the Departed," and begins with a call that inclines in wonder:

> O the nocturnal wing-beat of the soul:

The line ends with a colon that includes everything that follows, even to the transition from descent into ascent. At that point in the poem, just before the last two lines, there is a

second colon. Then follows the simple phrase "*One* generation." The word "One" is stressed. As far as I can see it is the
only word so stressed in Trakl's work. This emphatic "*one*
generation" contains the key note in which Trakl's poetic
work silently sounds the mystery. The unity of the *one* kinship
arises from the race which, along "the lunar paths of the
departed," gathers together and enfolds the discord of the
generations into the gentler two-fold—which does so in virtue
of its apartness, the stiller stillness reigning within it, in virtue
of its "forest sagas," its "measure and law."

The "*one*" in "*one* generation" does not mean one as opposed
to two. Nor does it mean the monotony of dull equality. "*One*
generation" here does not refer to a biological fact at all, to a
"single" or "identical" gender. In the emphatic "*one* generation" there is hidden that unifying force which unifies in virtue
of the ghostly night's gathering blue. The word speaks from the
song which sings of evening. Accordingly, the word "generation" here retains the full manifold meaning mentioned earlier.
For one thing, it names the historical generation of man, mankind as distinct from all other living beings (plants and
animals) . Next, the word "generation" names the races, tribes,
clans, and families of mankind. At the same time, the word
always refers to the twofoldness of the sexes.

The force which marks the tribes of mankind as the simple
oneness of "*one* generation," and thus restores them and mankind itself to the stiller childhood, acts by prompting the soul
to set out toward the "blue spring." The soul sings of the blue
spring by keeping it silent. The poem "In the Dark" (144)
begins:

> The soul keeps the blue spring in silence.

"Keep silent" is here used transitively. Trakl's poem sings of
the land of evening. It is one single call that the right race may
come to be, and to speak the flame of the spirit into gentleness.
In the "Kaspar Hauser Song" (109) we read how God addressed Kaspar Hauser:

> God spoke a gentle flame to his heart:
> O man!

The "spoke," too, is used transitively here, just as "keeps" was above, or as "bleeds" in "To the Boy Elis" (91), or "murmurs" in the last line of "On the Mönchsberg" (107).

God's speaking is the speaking which assigns to man a stiller nature, and so calls on him to give that response by which man rises from what is authentic ruin up into earliness. The "evening land" holds the rising of the dawn of the "*one* generation."

How shallow is our thinking if we regard the singer of the "Occidental Song" as the poet of decay. How incomplete and crude is our understanding if we insist on approaching Trakl's other poem, "Evening Land" (165), always only in terms of its final third section, while stubbornly ignoring the center piece of the triptych together with its preparation in the first section. In "Evening Land" the Elis figure appears once again, whereas "Helian" and "Sebastian in Dream" are no longer mentioned in the last poems. The stranger's footfalls resound. They resound in harmony with the "softly sounding spirit" of the ancient forest legend. The final section—where the "mighty cities/ stone on stone raised up/ in the plain!" are mentioned— is already overcome, absorbed into the middle section of this work. The cities already have their destiny. It is a destiny other than that which is spoken "beside the greening hill" where the "spring storm sings," the hill which has its "just measure" (128) and is also called the "evening hill" (143). It has been said that Trakl's work is "profoundly unhistorical." In this judgment, what is meant by history? If the word means no more than "chronicle," the rehearsal of past events, then Trakl is indeed unhistorical. His poetry has no need of historical "objects." Why not? Because his poetic work is historical in the highest sense. His poetry sings of the destiny which casts mankind in its still withheld nature—that is to say, saves mankind.

Trakl's work sings the song of the soul, "something strange on the earth," which is only just about to gain the earth by its wandering, the earth that is the stiller home of the homecoming generation.

Is this dreamy romanticism, at the fringe of the technically-economically oriented world of modern mass existence? Or—is it the clear knowledge of the "madman" who sees and senses other things than the reporters of the latest news who spend themselves chronicling the current happening, whose future is never more than a prolongation of today's events, a future that is forever without the advent of a destiny which concerns man for once at the source of his being?

The poet sees the soul, "something strange," destined to follow a path that leads not to decay, but on the contrary to a going under. This going under yields and submits to the mighty death in which he who died early leads the way. The brother, singing, follows him in death. Following the stranger, the dying friend passes through the ghostly night of the years of apartness. His singing is the "Song of a Captured Blackbird," a poem dedicated to L. v. Ficker. The blackbird is the bird that called Elis to go under. It is the birdvoice of the deathlike one. The bird is captured in the solitude of the golden footfalls that correspond to the ride of the golden boat on which Elis' heart crosses the blue night's starry pond, and thus shows to the soul the course of its essential being.

> Something strange is the soul on the earth.

The soul journeys toward the land of evening, which is pervaded by the spirit of apartness and is, in keeping with that spirit, "ghostly."

All formulas are dangerous. They force whatever is said into the superficiality of instant opinion and are apt to corrupt our thinking. But they may also be of help, at least as a prompting and a starting point for sustained reflection. With these reservations, we may venture this formulation:

A discussion of the site of Georg Trakl's poetic work shows him to be the poet of the yet concealed evening land.

> Something strange is the soul on the earth.

The sentence occurs in the poem "Springtime of the Soul" (142 f.). The verse that leads over into that final stanza where the sentence belongs, runs:

> Mighty dying and the singing flame in the heart.

There follows the rising of the song into the pure echo of the music of the ghostly years, through which the stranger wanders, the years which the brother follows who begins dwelling in the land of evening:

> Darker the waters flowed round the lovely games of
>   the fishes.
> Hour of mourning and silent sight of the sun;
> Something strange is the soul on the earth. Ghostly
>   the twilight
> Bluing over the mishewn forest, and a dark bell
> Long tolls in the village; they lead him to rest.
> Silent the myrtle blooms over his dead white eyelids.
>
> Softly murmur the waters in the declining afternoon,
> On the banks the green wilderness darkens, joy in the
>   rosy wind;
> The gentle song of the brother by the evening hill.

REFERENCES

[The German volume *Unterwegs zur Sprache* here translated also contains an essay entitled *Die Sprache* (Language) which has here been omitted by arrangement with the author, and will be found in translation elsewhere in Martin Heidegger, *Poetry, Language, Thought* (Harper & Row, 1971).]

A DIALOGUE ON LANGUAGE

The heretofore unpublished text originated in 1953/54, on the occasion of a visit by Professor Tezuka of the Imperial University, Tokyo.

To counter widely circulated allegations, let it be stated here explicitly that the dedication of *Being and Time* mentioned on page 16 of the *Dialogue* remained in *Being and Time* until its fourth edition of 1935. In 1941, when my publishers felt that the fifth edition might be endangered and that, indeed, the book might be suppressed, it was finally agreed, on the suggestion and at the desire of Niemeyer, that the dedication be omitted from the edition, on the condition imposed by me that the note to page 38 be retained—a note which in fact states the reason for that dedication, and which runs: "If the following investigation has taken any steps forward in disclosing the 'things themselves', the author must first of all thank E. Husserl, who, by providing his own incisive personal guidance and by freely turning over his unpublished investigations, familiarized the author with the most diverse areas of phenomenological research during his student years in Freiburg" (*Being and Time,* Harper & Row, 1962, p. 489).

Concerning the "two-fold" mentioned in the *Dialogue,* compare *What Is Called Thinking?* (Harper & Row, 1968) and *Identity and Difference* (Harper & Row, 1969).

THE NATURE OF LANGUAGE

The three lectures were delivered in the *studium generale* of the University of Freiburg i. Br. on the 4th and the 18th of December, 1957, and on February 7, 1958.

THE WAY TO LANGUAGE

This lecture is part of a lecture series on the subject "Language" which was arranged, in January 1959, by the Bavarian Academy of the Fine Arts and the Academy of the Arts in Berlin.

The text has been revised for publication and, in a few places, enlarged. It first appeared in print in the Fourth Series of *Gestalt und Gedanke,* 1959 (ed. Clemens Graf Podewils).

WORDS

The text in its present version was first delivered as a lecture, during a matinee celebration, at the *Burgtheater* in Vienna, under the title *Dichten und Denken. Zu Stefan Georges Gedicht* Das Wort.

LANGUAGE IN THE POEM

This essay first appeared in *Merkur,* 1953, No. 61, pp. 226-258, under the title: *George Trakl. Eine Erörterung seines Gedichtes.*